NIGHT FIGHTER ACES OF THE LUFTWAFFE 1940–43

CASEMATE | ILLUSTRATED

CASEMATE | ILLUSTRATED

NIGHT FIGHTER ACES OF THE LUFTWAFFE 1940–43

NEIL PAGE AND JEAN-LOUIS ROBA

CASEMATE | ILLUSTRATED

CIS0050

Published in 2025 by
CASEMATE PUBLISHERS
1950 Lawrence Road, Havertown, PA 19083, USA
and
47 Church Street, Barnsley, S70 2AS, UK

Print Edition: ISBN 978 1 63624 490 7
Digital Edition: ISBN 978-1-63624-491-4

Design by Battlefield Design
Aircraft profiles by Claes Sundin
Printed and bound in the Czech Republic by FINIDR s.r.o.

CASEMATE PUBLISHERS (US)
Telephone (610) 853-9131
Fax (610) 853-9146
Email: casemate@casematepublishers.com
www.casematepublishers.com

CASEMATE PUBLISHERS (UK)
Telephone (0)1226 734350
Email: casemate@casemateuk.com
www.casemateuk.com

Photo credits: From the collections of Jean-Louis Roba, Neil Page, Peter Taghon, Roland Charlier, Theo Boiten, Paul Stipdonk, Delmar Davis, and Michael Meyer.

Title page: A rare Dornier Do 17 Z-10 on the strength of NJG 2 in the fall of 1941.

Contents page: In Scandinavia a special detachment of Ju 88 Cs was assigned to the Adlergeschwader to form a Staffel, (Z)./KG 30, tasked with attempting to intercept British bombers at night.

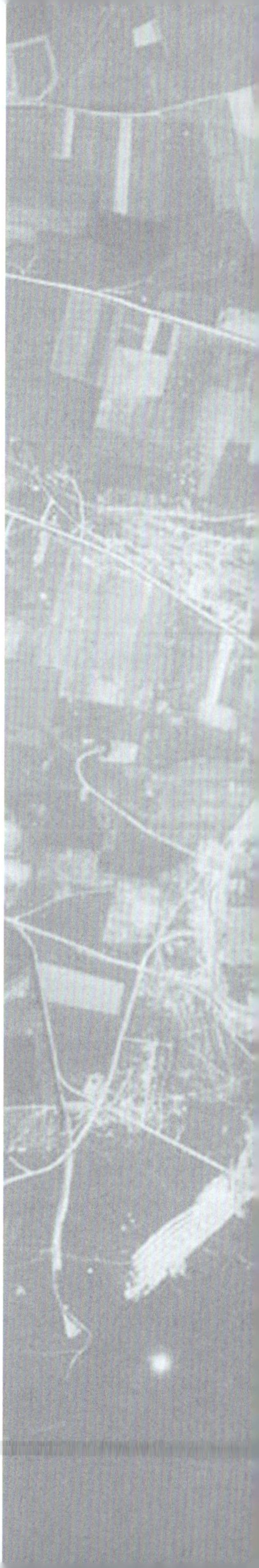

Contents

Timeline of Events 6
Introduction 8
Origins of the Luftwaffe Night Fighter Arm 10
The Nachtjagd Evolves: January–June 1941 23
Piercing the Darkness: July–December 1941 38
Enter "Bomber" Harris: January–June 1942 52
Luftsiege Mount: July–December 1942 75
Battle for the Ruhr: January–June 1943 89
Wilde Sau: Summer 1943 105
Afterword 124
References and Further Reading 125
Index 126

Timeline of Events

The Luftwaffe's Nachtjagd grew from Wolfgang Falck's frustration at not being able to chase down RAF bombers at night. However, in short time it grew into a chain of radar stations, searchlight batteries, and command posts between England and northwest Germany, the so-called defensive "line" named after the commander of Germany's nighttime fighter defenses, Josef Kammhuber. But continually bedeviled by a lack of resources such as adequate aircraft and experienced crews, the Nachtjagd was to spend much of its life playing catchup. And despite the Freya, Lichtenstein, and Würzburg radar systems, RAF Bomber Command always seemed one step ahead in terms of jamming capabilities. Added to that, the introduction of the "Window" chaff tactic played havoc with the Nachtjagd's ability to even find its prey, coupled with the vast bomber "streams" that saturated the skies over Germany. The one technological development that did give the Nachtjagd the edge was the upward-firing cannon, *Schräge Musik*. Tactically, *Wilde Sau* did not rely on radar and could obviate the RAF's jamming capability. German night fighters accounted for about 60 percent of Bomber Command's nighttime losses.

September 1, 1939: Germany invades Poland.

September 3, 1939: Britain and France declare war on Germany.

October 1939–April 1940: The "Phoney War."

April 9, 1940: Operation *Weserübung* lays the foundations for the Nachtjagd.

May 10, 1940: Hitler launches his Blitzkrieg against the Low Countries and France.

May 15/16, 1940: 81 RAF bombers strike the Ruhr.

June 22, 1940: Falck takes over the new Nachtjagdgeschwader 1.

August 25/26, 1940: RAF bombs Berlin.

July 10–October 31, 1940: The Battle of Britain.

Bf 110 C/D "G9+AM" flown by Oblt. Walter Barte, Staffelkapitän of 4./NJG 1 during early 1941. Barte survived the war with 23 victories in NJG 1 and 3.

February 1941: The Afrika Korps is deployed to North Africa.

April 6–June 1941: Germany invades the Balkans.

June 22, 1941: Operation *Barbarossa*, the invasion of the USSR.

February 7, 1942: British commandos capture a Würzburg radar at Bruneval.

May 30/31, 1942: First RAF "1,000-bomber raid," against Cologne.

June 1/2, 1942: Heinz Schnaufer returns the first of his record 121 nighttime *Abschüsse*.

October 23, 1942: Battle of El Alamein.

February 2, 1943: German defeat at Stalingrad.

March 5/6–July 24, 1943: Bomber Command conducts the "battle of the Ruhr."

May 9, 1943: Ju 88 R-1 "D5+EV" defects to RAF Dyce in Scotland.

July 3/4, 1943: First successful *Wilde Sau* interception accounts for 12 RAF bombers.

July 27/28, 1943: Deadly RAF *Feuersturm* (firestorm) bombing raid against Hamburg.

Introduction

Veulen is a small village in the municipality of Venray just off the Ijsselstein exit along the Duisberg–Eindhoven Autobahn in Limburg, in the southeastern corner of the Netherlands. Mostly just fields and woods. There is a large holiday campsite to the southwest. Some 20 miles to the southeast, almost on the border with Germany, is the town of Venlo. Yet in Veulen and its environs many hundreds of German servicemen and women served out World War II—at least until September 1944. Veulen was home to the night fighter control center (or Nachtjagdgefechtsstand) for area "Raum 5B," part of a chain of radar stations, searchlight batteries, and command posts between England and northwest Germany, the so-called defensive "line" named after the commander of Germany's nighttime fighter defenses, Kammhuber.

Veulen directed the night fighters that were based on the huge night fighter base that was constructed in Venlo in the wake of the first RAF nighttime bombing raids of Germany's industrial area, the Ruhr, from mid-1940. From October 1940, Luftwaffe construction teams employing thousands of Dutch workers expanded the *Hilfslandeplatz* (auxiliary airfield) at Venlo into an airfield complex of almost 1,800 hectares, with three runways, 48 kilometers of roads and taxiways, and over 100 aircraft dispersals and hangars. It was the biggest Luftwaffe night fighter airfield in Holland and was occupied by the black-camouflaged night fighters of I./NJG 1 under their Kommandeur Hptm. Werner Streib even before its completion in March 1941. It was from here during the spring of 1943 that Streib conducted the first successful combat trials of the Heinkel He 219, the first "specialist" Luftwaffe night fighter.

At first sight the German night fighter arm, the Nachtjagd, was able to quickly develop after the initial trials flown with Bf 110s at dusk during late April 1940 in Aalborg, Denmark. However, there were no purpose-built night-fighting aircraft, tactics or procedures, much less night fighter bases. In short, resources and personnel were lacking. After the establishment of NJG 1, 1. Nachtjagd.Division (Night Fighter Division) was founded in the summer of 1940 under the-then Colonel (Oberst) Josef Kammhuber. With it came the establishment of further Nachtjagdgeschwader, but only gradually from March 1941. By then the first Kommodore of NJG 1 was in charge of as many as eight night fighter Staffeln. NJG 1 was the "mother" Geschwader of the Luftwaffe night fighter arm and from its ranks came virtually all the later Kommodoren, Gruppenkommandeure, and many of the Staffelkapitäne.

The fledgling Nachtjagd was quickly caught up in a struggle for technological supremacy, triggered and then accelerated by the RAF. Within two years of sending isolated raiders over Germany during the Battle of Britain, the RAF could deploy well over 1,000 bomber aircraft on nighttime raids. For the Germans actual night-fighting began as "illuminated night hunting" in cooperation with the Flak and searchlight batteries. This was followed by various phases of "guided" night-fighting. Ground command posts plotted bombers and night fighters through the night sky divided into "boxes"—the so-called "*Himmelbett*" or "four-poster bed" method with its four elements. At the same time, long-range night intruder operations over England were in full swing to disrupt RAF bombers departing on missions and arriving home after raids over Germany. Both these approaches would fall from favor.

By early 1943 the RAF had an accurate bomb aiming and navigation sytem (Oboe). The RAF's Pathfinder Force deployed Oboe-equipped Mosquitos carrying special target markers, enabling bombing even where targets were obscured by thick cloud cover. The bombers themselves had ground-mapping H2S radar and increasingly in many instances Monica tail-warning radar. German technicians regularly shifted through the wrecks of RAF bombers looking for new electronic devices and clues on how they might be countered. The Nachtjagd did develop one notable "technical" modification that the RAF failed to counter—the deadly upward-firing cannon codenamed *Schräge Musik*. But while growing numbers of Luftwaffe fighters bristling with cannon and stag-antler radar antennae shot down numbers of RAF bombers, only a relatively small group of German "aces" achieved kills at night, a tendency exacerbated by deploying the high-scoring aces to key locations. The rest, consigned to their "boxes" and only deployed after the "first wave," never even saw an RAF bomber. Their aircraft—even the specialist night fighter variants—were essentially the same machines the Luftwaffe had gone to war with and were barely any faster than their prey. As RAF raids grew in intensity, there were considerable "political" difficulties for those charged with Germany's nighttime defenses as they sought to deploy ever more costly infrastructure and new specialist night fighter aircraft types into Luftwaffe service.

In the end Kammhuber's "system" was brought down by RAF jamming of German radar over Hamburg in July 1943. Fortunately for the Germans the so-called "*Wilde Sau*" procedure was being actively tested during the spring of 1943 with single-engined night fighters operating independently of radar control and directly over cities and towns under attack.

By this time the Nachtjagd had developed into arguably the most modern branch of the Luftwaffe and by the end of the war this purely "defensive" arm had claimed well over 6,000 victories, with NJG 1 alone responsible for some 2,000 of these for the loss of over 700 airmen.

Origins of the Luftwaffe Night Fighter Arm

During the Great War, aerial combat also took place at night, mainly in the face of Zeppelin and heavy German bomber (Gotha or Halberstadt) attacks on London and Paris. Some successes were achieved but, despite these efforts, night-fighting remained very limited and was little appreciated after 1918. While the creation of an offensive air arm took place covertly in the interwar period, the nascent Luftwaffe was largely geared towards tactical and offensive actions in support of fast-moving ground forces (Blitzkrieg). Nachtjagd—night-fighting—was not a priority.

Of course, the Generalstab der Luftwaffe was not blind—the Condor Legion in Spain flew many nighttime bombing raids with Ju 52s. At least two of these trimotors were intercepted by Republican fighters and shot down. However, it failed to understand that the RAF had laid the foundations for a strategic bomber force long before the start of World War II. Following the failure of the Geneva disarmament conference in July 1934—Hitler had already withdrawn Germany from the League of Nations and de facto revised the terms of the Treaty of Versailles—Germany was recognized as a potential major threat. The only possibility for the British of striking at Germany was likely to be through aerial bombardment by bomber aircraft in accordance with the theories of General Giulio Douhet, an early advocate of strategic bombing. Back in the 1920s the first Marshal of the Royal Air Force, Hugh Trenchard, was a proponent—he firmly believed that the future belonged to large fleets of bombers, albeit operating by day.

The first "strategic" RAF bombing raids on Germany took place as a response to the German invasion of the Low Countries and France—during the night of May 15/16, 1940, 81 bombers unloaded their cargoes over the Ruhr. On the night of June 4/5 some 50 RAF bombers, either operating alone or in small groups, again bombed several targets in Germany. Berlin was bombed for the first time by the RAF on the night of August 25/26, 1940.

While the night defense of Germany was neglected, it did exist to a limited extent. On May 1, 1939, at Döberitz, outdated Arado Ar 68s and a few Bf 109 Ds were brought together to form a 10.(N)/JG 2 under the command of an Oblt. Müller. The Staffel soon moved to Brandenburg-Briest and then to Jever. A 10.(N)/JG 72 also existed for a short period. Following the invasion of Poland on September 1, 1939, another "night-fighting" Staffel, 10.(N)/JG 26, was formed at Bonn-Hangelar with the same equipment. Commanded by Oblt. Johannes Steinhoff, it soon moved to Stade and Jever. Assigned to defend the strategic Bay of Germany, the Bf 109s (having replaced the obsolescent Arados) initially operated mainly by day, with 10.(N)/JG 26 being credited with no fewer than six Wellington bombers during the "famous" air battle of December 18, 1939 flown against north German ports. These increasingly heavy losses during daylight missions forced RAF Bomber Command to give priority to night bombing. In February 1940, to counter this change in tactics, 10.(N)/JG 26 was redesignated 11.(N)/JG 2, with a 12. Staffel added to form V.(N)/JG 2 commanded by Hptm. Albert Blumensaat. On February 23, 1940, Ofw. Hermann Förster (11.) was credited with a Wellington near Nordeney, but this was also during the day.

On April 9, 1940, Operation *Weserübung* was launched, indirectly laying the foundations for the Nachtjagd. 11 Staffel of JG 2 flew into Aalborg and, on the night of April 25/26, Förster scored his second victory over a Hampden of 49 Sqn, the first night victory by a German fighter unit in the war.

The RAF was very active over Scandinavia, regularly attacking airfields at night. This particularly irritated Hptm. Wolfgang Falck, who had made his mark in ZG 76 during the fighting over the Bay of Germany but who was now in charge of I./ZG 1. As the British raids were only countered by very inaccurate Flak fire, Falck selected a few experienced pilots to test out his idea of using his Bf 110s as night fighters. As he recalled in his memoir:

> We had an excellent time in Aalborg. But after a while, RAF bombers were overhead more and more often, flying into Germany on night raids and returning overhead again at dawn. When they had bombs left over, they would jettison them on us or shoot at us with their weapons. Far too seldom one of them would be shot down by the antiaircraft defenses. Something had to be done. There was a radar monitoring position [*eine Funkmess-Stellung*] on the coast not far from the airbase. The Freya device, which was operated here under the command of a Leutnant named Werner Bode, was able to measure the direction and speed of the approaching and departing RAF bombers so we knew to the minute when they would appear overhead. This gave us the time we needed to evacuate the buildings before we were possibly attacked … I started to get annoyed with the British. If they could fly at night—why couldn't we? After all, we were also equipped with twin-engine aeroplanes and most of my pilots had been trained to fly on instruments [*Blindflugausbildung*].

During World War I, German Zeppelins and heavy bombers were often sent out on night raids, as in this drawing showing biplanes defending Paris under bombardment.

A press conference was held immediately after the December 18 air battle. Obstlt. Carl Schumacher (JG 1) chats with Reichspressechef Otto Dietrich, State Secretary in the Reich Ministry of Public Enlightenment and Propaganda while three of the successful pilots discuss tactics. From left: Oblt. Johannes Steinhoff of 11.(N)/JG 2, Oblt. Wolfgang Falck of I./ZG 76, and Oblt. Anton Pointner of 5./JG 77.

> So, I contacted the commander of the searchlight and Flak battery on the airfield and approached Lt. Bode about my ideas. My proposal to both was to set up a coordinated network over North Jutland, the Skagerrak, the Kattegat, and the eastern North Sea, which from now on would be monitored by the Freya radar, searchlights, Flak, and I./ZG 1. If Bode's Freya detected enemy flights encroaching on our grid, my Bf 110s would fly out to sea so that Flak and searchlights on site and in its vicinity would not have to take any notice of us. We would wait over the North Sea until the British bombers were close enough to us, according to Bode's returns, and then try to make visual contact and shoot them down. If the British stuck to their routines, they had to come through our surveillance zone at dawn on their return flight from the Reich: there would be enough natural light to make visual contact with them. Moreover, the nights were rarely so dark that you couldn't recognize an aircraft reasonably close by, even if it was only from its exhaust flames. *So begannen wir mit der Nachtjagd* … this was how we started night-fighting.

Falck continued:

> I initially selected three crews to find out with me how suitable the 110 really was for such missions—the pilots were Oblt. Werner Streib, Hptm. Günther Radusch, and Ofw. Thier. I estimated that along with myself these three had the most blind-flying experience. We flew our first practice sorties during spring 1940 and although Streib thought the idea of night-fighting crazy, Radusch, Thier, and I considered that it was possible. *Drei zu eins*—three to one. Werner Streib stuck to the "program," even if he wasn't convinced, and we continued to work on our

tactics. A few nights later—the night of April 30/May 1—the RAF once again hit our airfield, but the coordination between us and the other units involved didn't work out. The British were over the aerodrome in no time, dropped a few small bombs, hit our planes with their onboard armament, and disappeared, while we crawled out of our shrapnel trenches and manholes, cursing. Driven by impotent rage, we jumped into our Bf 110s and followed the bombers. We were neither strapped in nor wearing our flight helmets—we just thundered off without any radio communication and it was pure luck that none of us rolled headlong into a bomb crater on take off. With a clear night sky and relatively good visibility, we headed westward and after a few minutes I actually spotted a low-flying enemy aircraft. I fired at it from a distance, but as soon as the enemy noticed the attack, it dived into the early morning haze over the North Sea and disappeared. Fips Radusch also made contact with the enemy [*Feindberührung*] and attacked, but his prey eluded him in the same way as mine. He had even come so close to the bomber that he received defensive fire. Ofw. Thier was also able to attack a bomber and flew three firing passes—albeit also unsuccessfully. Werner Streib had seen nothing at all. That made it three to one again. There was basically something to our experiments, but we were still doing too much wrong. Step by step, we improved what was proving to be inadequate. Our Bf 110s were fitted with flame dampers for the exhausts of their Daimler-Benz engines so that we were no longer irritated by the constant blue-red sizzling of the exhaust flames, which were completely invisible during the day but dazzled us considerably at night, and made it easier for an enemy to spot and fire at us. We experimented with ammunition that both reduced the muzzle flash and shone less brightly in the trajectory than the usual tracer rounds. We supplemented the blind-flying instrumentation of our aircraft and racked our brains with the people from the Flak, searchlight, and radar positions about how to optimize our cooperation. Finally, I wrote a report with our recommendations and sent it to the Reich Aviation Ministry (Reichsluftfahrtministerium) and while we hoped for a reply, we continued to work on our ideas.

At Aalborg, a 109 of 11.(N)/JG 2 displays the owl (*Eule*) badge of the Night Fighter Staffel.

A Bf 109 D of 10(N)./JG 26 tested single-engine nighttime flying as early as September 1939. Note the *Eule* (owl) emblem on the engine cowl of "white 11." The folding section of the canopy was removed to cut down on reflections.

It was all very early days, but a great deal of experience was gained. Falck's report reached the desk of Reichsmarschall Hermann Göring where it was well received.

On May 10, 1940, the Wehrmacht launched its assault on the West. One element of the West's response was the dispatch of RAF Bomber Command "heavy" bombers (Wellington, Hampden, Whitley) at night over German industrial centers. These raids had only limited effect but exasperated the Germans who set out to create a credible night fighter force based on Falck's blueprint. On June 22, as the Western Campaign ended, the recently promoted Maj. Falck, who had persisted with his night-fighting trials and was already considered to be a "specialist," was appointed Kommodore of a new Nachtjagdgeschwader 1.

I./NJG 1 was entrusted to Hptm. Walter Radusch. The Gruppe was established through the expedient of "renaming" I./ZG 1 (Falck's old unit) equipped mainly with Bf 110s. The transfer took place at Münchengladbach. II./NJG 1 was led by Hptm. Conrad von Bothmer, who had flown in Spain (but had hardly distinguished himself there). This Gruppe was in fact made up of the Bf 109s of IV./JG 2 based at Amsterdam-Schiphol.

On the night of June 28/29, during one of the new unit's first engagements, a Do 17 of 1./NJG 1 was damaged near Münchengladbach.

Despite the solid German organization, the early days of NJG 1 were rather haphazard. On July 1, the brand-new II./NJG 1 became III./NJG 1; a second II./NJG 1 (Kdr: Hptm.

Discussion between I./ ZG 1 comrades in Aalborg, Denmark. From left: Oblt. Werner Streib, Oblt. Walter Ehle, and Lt. Helmut Schwabedissen. While the latter was killed in France on May 17, 1940, his two comrades became Nachtjagd aces.

In Scandinavia, a few other attempts were made to intercept British bombers at night. A special detachment of Ju 88 Cs was assigned to the Adlergeschwader to form a Staffel, (Z)./KG 30.

Karl-Heinrich Heyse) was created, with 4./NJG 1 being the former (Z)/KG 30 and 5./NJG 1 a renaming of 1./NJG 1, while 6./NJG 1 was formed with young recruits. It should be noted that Heyse, a veteran of the Condor Legion, was initially a bomber pilot; 10./ZG 26 was redesignated 1./NJG 1.

After all these hasty changes, which brought NJG 1 up to full strength, the Geschwader was deployed as follows in July 1940: Stab/NJG 1: Deelen (Bf 110); I./NJG 1: Gütersloh (Bf 110/Do 17); II./NJG 1: Düsseldorf (Ju 88); III./NJG 1: Düsseldorf (Bf 109 E).

In August, III./NJG 1 gradually replaced its "Emils" with more suitable Bf 110s. The Bf 109s then formed 10. and 11./NJG 1 but were certainly not used much.

A Bf 110 of the Stab III./NJG 1. The first Bf 109s assigned to this Gruppe were progressively supplanted by the Bf 110 twin-engined heavy fighters displaying the NJG 1 codes "G9."

The "Englandblitz" Nachtjagd Emblem

The "Englandblitz" badge with its lightning bolts striking at England was adopted by all night fighter units as well as several Nachtjagd support units. Paradoxically, however, it was originally the badge of a Zerstörer (destroyer) unit, Wolfgang Falck's I./ZG 1. As he recalled in *Jägerblatt:*

When I was appointed Kommandeur of I.Gruppe in Zerstörergeschwader 1 in Düsseldorf in the spring of 1940, I quickly realized—based on my experience as a Staffelkapitän in the "Marienkäfer Staffel"—that a badge or an emblem is not only an outward sign of a unit's solidarity, but can also be of great psychological and educational value. Based on this realization, I called on all members of I./ZG 1 to make suggestions for a Gruppe badge. Of the various designs I liked the sketch by the-then Oblt. Viktor Mölders most especially; the badge, in the form of a coat of arms, showed a segment of the globe encompassing our operational area, from Norway via Denmark, Germany to the French Atlantic coast, including England, on which a white falcon—taken from my family crest—swooped down with a red lightning bolt, the tip of which struck the ground in southern England. This was symbolic of our mission, as the RAF was our only enemy at the time. No sooner had I decided on this badge than in June 1940 in Wassenar I was ordered to form Night Fighter Wing 1 from my Gruppe and a fighter Gruppe in the Rhineland equipped with 109s. I became Kommodore of this Geschwader while still only with the rank of Hptm. It was a simple enough matter to "modify" our new Gruppe emblem to reflect this new mission by changing its sky background to black with a white outline—the red, white, and black with the white diving falcon were all on my family coat of arms. We saw it as a symbol of our commitment and our willingness to fight, while in the eyes of the Party the emblem featured the *Siegesrune* victory runes, so the badge was introduced without objection. It was not only displayed on the aircraft, but also on all the Geschwader vehicles. When night fighter operations were intensified and new Geschwader formed as part of the division and later the XII Flieger-Korps, this insignia remained valid for all other units with minor symbolic changes, e.g., NJG 1 had a white border, NJG 2 a red border, and NJG 3 a yellow border. The Flak searchlight regiments symbolically added a few searchlight beams and the air signals regiments added their radio emblem. The emblem even featured in the postwar Federal German air force with minor modifications as the badge of 1. Staffel of Jagdgeschwader 74—in the early 1960s their F-86K jets were the only aircraft flying nighttime IFR sorties.

Viktor Mölders, Werner Streib's gunner/radio operator, designed the Englandblitz emblem but did not go on to serve in the Nachtjagd.

Up until around 1943 all Luftwaffe night fighters were painted black—black was generally considered to be a non-reflective color. However, black aircraft were vulnerable to both observation from above (especially when silhouetted against clouds illuminated from the ground) and observation from below, especially standing out against a lighter sky.

On July 5, the first serious loss for NJG 1 occurred when a Ju 88 C-2 of 4. Staffel (ex-Z/KG 30) was shot down near Karstädt. Two of the crew were able to jump clear, but the pilot was killed. It is surprising how few casualties were reported at the time, when flying at night was particularly dangerous. But Falck, as a good organizer, had undoubtedly ordered the most experienced crews to be retained, with the airmen who were either unfit or unwilling to fight at night (like Viktor Mölders?) being transferred to other units.

On the night of July 19/20, Oblt. Werner Streib, Staka of 2./NJG 1, shot down a Whitley of 51 Sqn at Ibbenbüren, thus scoring the first nighttime victory credited to a Bf 110. Ofw. Hermann Förster of 5./NJG 1 had returned the first officially credited night victory for NJG 1 in downing a 10 Sqn Whitley during the night of July 8/9

More victories then followed in quick succession. On July 20/21, Oblt. Walter Ehle and Siegfried Wandam shot down two Wellingtons; on July 21/22, Streib downed a Whitley (two claims by two other pilots have not been identified); on July 25/26, another Wellington was shot down by a crew from 3./NJG 1.

August saw four claims (but only two of Streib's victories can be identified). At the outset, the German night fighters were deployed on the so-called "illuminated night-fighting" or *Helle Nachtjagd* tactic, operating in close cooperation with the searchlight batteries. These "coned" the British bombers, guiding the fighters towards their prey. The guns stopped firing as the Nachtjäger approached, but often the bombers escaped the searchlights and flew off into the darkness. The crews of Bomber Command particularly feared nights lit up when the moon was full.

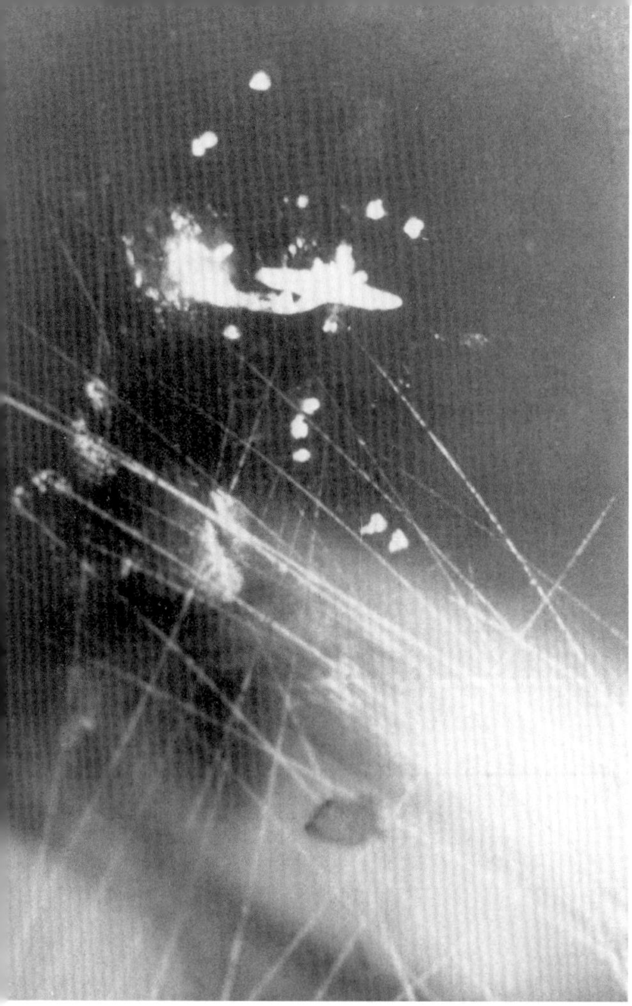

An example of *Helle Nachtjagd* in action. A Wellington is "coned" by searchlight beams and can be easily spotted by a nearby night fighter.

September 1, 1940 saw a major reinforcement when II./NJG 1 became I./NJG 2, a "special" unit coded "4R+." Equipped with long-range "heavy fighters," this Gruppe was tasked with "intruder" missions over England to attack RAF bombers at source, a tactic conceived by Kammhuber. As he put it: "When I have to destroy a wasps' nest, I don't attack the wasps one by one but wait until they have all returned to the nest to smoke them out."

This so-called *Fernnachtjagd* (long-range night hunting) was very ambitious and apparently promising, but its application was to prove more uncertain. Maj. Heyse's three Staffeln were highly diverse: 1./NJG 2: Oblt. Herbert Bönsch had led the Zerstörerstaffel of KG 30 before taking command of 4/NJG 1. His squadron consisted of a single Ju 88 C-1; 2./NJG 2: Hptm. Rudolf "Rolf" Jung was an ex-Staka of 2./ZG 2. The Staffel was equipped with Do 17 Z-7s and Z-10s, and a few Ju 88s; 3./NJG 2: Hptm. Karl-Theodor "Kurt" Hülshoff was an ex-Staka of 7./KG 54, then 6./NJG 1. The Staffel flew Ju 88 C-2s.

Exceptionally, to carry out its risky operations, I./NJG 2 had a 4. Staffel raised on the basis of 1./ZG 2. It was led by Oblt. Paul Bohn and equipped with Ju 88s.

A 2./NJG 2 Do 17 Z-10 in Gilze-Rijen.

As II./NJG 1 had become I./NJG 2, I./ZG 76 was designated as the new II./NJG 1. I./ZG 76 was a Zerstörer unit which had fought in Poland and Scandinavia and had several young aces on the pilot roster including Lt. Helmut Lent, who already had seven day victories to his name.

On 8 September, I./NJG 2 moved from Schiphol to Gilze-Rijen.

To compensate for the loss of this Gruppe, NJG 1 integrated I./ZG 76 (Kdr: Hptm. Graf von Stillfried und Rattonitz) which became II./NJG 1 and left Scandinavia to establish itself at Deelen. On September 7, 3./NJG 1 moved to Deelen to become 4./NJG 1, a new 3./NJG 1 being formed on the basis of 1./ZG 76.

While NJG 1 operated on the continent, I./NJG 2 began its first missions over England, with all the risks that this entailed. On September 7, Oblt. Kurt Herrmann (4./NJG 2) claimed a Blenheim near Waddington, but there is no trace of this, nor of the Blenheim confirmed downed on September 9 to Fw. Hermann Sommer. On September 16, the Gruppe suffered its first serious loss when a Ju 88 of 3./NJG 2 was hit by antiaircraft fire and crashed into the sea with its crew. For its part, NJG 1 claimed around 10 victories while losing three aircraft for various reasons.

In October, III./NJG 1 finally parted with its handful of Bf 109s that were no longer of much use. They were sent to Vlissingen (Flushing) to reinforce Jagdstaffel Holland (soon to become 1./JG 1).

On October 1, probably to reward Maj. Falck for having set up NJG 1 so quickly, he was awarded a Ritterkreuz.

On October 6, Walter Radusch left the command of I./NJG 1 and moved to Vechta to take charge of the new I./NJG 3, the redesignated V. (Z)/LG 1 equipped with Bf 110s. This future Geschwader was given the code "D5+." I./NJG 1 thus came under the command of another great ace, Maj. Streib, who was awarded the Ritterkreuz on the same day. Kommandeur von Stillfried und Rattonitz was killed on the 6th after his aircraft suffered an engine fire, and his II./NJG 1 was taken over the next day by Maj. Walter Ehle.

On October 6, 1940, Streib (left) and Falck received the Ritterkreuz.

Seen here with his radio operator is the new Kommandeur of II./NJG 1, Maj. Walter Ehle, appointed in early October 1940. Note the aircraft displays the roman numeral "II."

Winter weather slowed activity on both sides, but NJG 1 claimed half a dozen victories in October while losing some six Bf 110s for various reasons (one shot down in combat with a bomber). During this month, I./NJG 2 could be credited with three confirmed victories and two aircraft losses without loss of life.

On November 1, Hptm. von Bothmer (who had been relieved of his command for disciplinary reasons) committed suicide. His III./NJG 1 was taken over for a short time by Hptm. Gerhard Schön.

On the night of November 16/17, 1940, the young Egmont Prinz zur Lippe-Weissenfeld achieved his first victory. He was to become a prominent *Experte* (ace).

In November, NJG 1 won only one victory, but it was the first for a future ace, Oblt. Egmont Prinz zur Lippe-Weissenfeld. Over the North Sea, I./NJG 2 claimed three victories but lost four aircraft and three crews, including that of its Kommandeur Heyse. The Gruppe was then taken over by Hptm. Hülshoff. NJG 3 was first mentioned in the casualty lists when a Bf 110 from 1. Staffel crashed with its crew during a *Helle Nachtjagd* exercise using searchlights.

In December, the NJG was again awarded only one *Luftsieg* (air victory). Two of its aircraft were lost, including one from the Erg. Staffel, the training squadron. For its part, the I./NJG 2 claimed four dubious victories while losing two crews.

At the end of 1940, it was already possible to draw up a first mostly mixed "balance sheet" for the newly established night-fighting arm of the Luftwaffe: NJG 1, led by competent airmen under Maj. Falck, was beginning to gain experience in the *Helle Nachtjagd* process while awaiting the development of night fighter detection and guidance systems.

At Gilze-Rijen, Hptm. Kurt Hülshoff, the second Kommandeur of I./NJG 2, welcomes Feldmarschall Albert Kesselring, who had come to visit the unit in December 1940.

In late 1940 in Arnhem, Kommodore Falck welcomes a shot-down RAF crew to his HQ in the Netherlands.

I./NJG 2 flying long-range *Fernnachtjagd* sorties over England suffered losses for a result that we now know to be rather disappointing. Their tactic of prowling around British airfields, with no means of guidance, at a time when the British were continually reinforcing their increasingly effective defenses (with antiaircraft batteries and more modern night fighters such as the Beaufighter) was of dubious value.

I./NJG 3 was in full formation.

Pilots of 2. Staffel of NJG 1 pictured in the winter of 1940/41 in front of a 1939 Ford Mercury 8 decorated with the "Englandblitz" NJG emblem. From left are Lt. Reinhold Knacke (RK July 1, 1942 and Eichenlaub February 7, 1943, 44 "kills"), Lt. Kurt Loos (DKiG, August 21, 1942 and a tally of 10 *Abschüsse*), Lt. Wolfgang "Ameise" Thimmig (Staka 2./NJG 1, DKiG July 12, 1943, 23 victories), Lt. Hermann Reese (Ehrenpokal, 5 *Abschüsse*), and Lt. Hans-Dieter Frank (RK June 20, 1943 and Eichenlaub, March 1944, a tally of 55 *Abschüsse*).

The Nachtjagd Evolves: January–June 1941

As usual, the winter largely froze out aerial action. However, during this period of calm, each side was able to refine its weapons. Bomber Command trained its crews in the new tactics and recent German weaponry while increasing its offensive potential by committing more powerful bombers (Stirling, Halifax, and Manchester). For its part, the Luftwaffe had appointed Ob. Josef Kammhuber to put the Nachtjagd on a solid footing by organizing its ground operations.

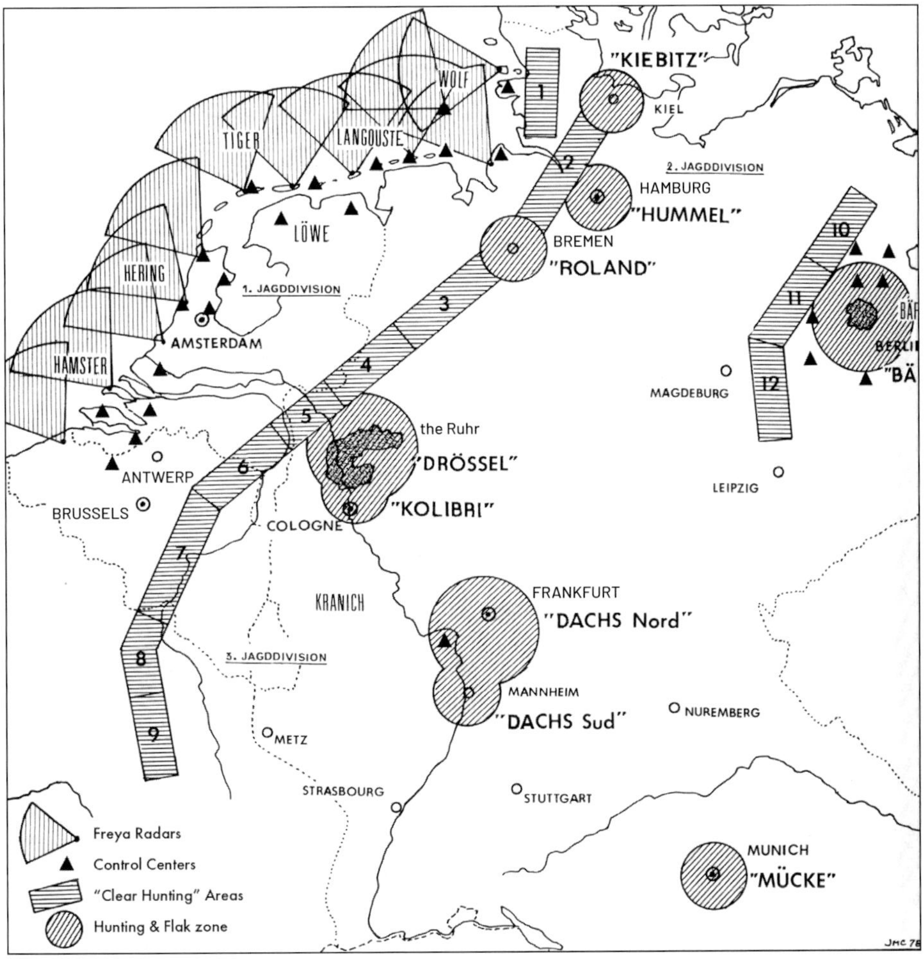

A sketch of the so-called Kammhuber Line.

German factories were to produce more and more Freya-type detection devices, which were scattered along the coasts and installed in strategic locations. They were used to predict the arrival of bombers, which put the warning system on the defensive. Kammhuber had in fact created a defensive belt that ran from the north of Germany to the north of France (but which could not be extended for lack of resources). This protective area, which came to be known as the "Kammhuber Line" ensured the protection of the industrial heartland of the Reich: the Ruhr, as well as major cities such as Hamburg, Berlin, and Frankfurt am Main. It was divided into various sectors (*Raum*) patrolled by night fighters who were deployed in turn during British raids. Each sector was equipped with increasingly sophisticated detection equipment and numerous Flak searchlights. As it was obvious that many bombers would cross this line, the ground defense fell to the Flak, which was widely deployed around the strategic targets. The Bf 110 crews gradually refined their approach and "hunting" tactics.

In January 1941, I./NJG 3 was hardly active, losing several aircraft during exercises. NJG 1 was left to defend the continent on its own. However, it only scored two victories that month. I./NJG 2 was luckier, with three victories for the loss of a single crew.

February saw the first victory for I./NJG 3: a Whitley from 77 Sqn shot down in the Netherlands by Oblt. Hans Jüsgens on the night of the 15th/16th. Two *Luftsiege* were obtained by NJG 1 but the unit lost two Bf 110s: one for lack of fuel and another shot down by Wunstorf's Flak. Attacking British bombers targeted by Flak could cause disasters. Over England, the I./NJG 2 achieved three definite victories (see textbox) but lost three crews on these far-flung and perilous missions.

The Nachtjagd was about to be weakened in Western Europe when, in February, 1/NJG 3 was sent to Sicily to support the X. Fliegerkorps and, if necessary, General Erwin Rommel's new Deutsche Afrika Korps (see below).

Losses did not only occur in combat. On February 18, Bf 110 D-3 "G9+HN" of 5./NJG 1 overturned at Deelen following a tire burst. Pilot Lt. Harras Matthes was killed.

Eight Victories in One Night

According to a report probably compiled for the propaganda services by an anonymous NJG 1 staff officer:

> The night of February 10/11, 1941 was crowned with renewed and important successes for our night fighters. Hptm. Ehle who had taken off on a *Dunkelnachtjagd* sortie opened the victory scoring list. At an altitude of 4,000 meters west of Nunspeet his Bordfunker Ofw. Wenk had suddenly sighted a Wellington in the moonlight cruising over the cloud deck 1,000 meters below them. He quickly drew the pilot's attention to the enemy aircraft and Ehle lost no time in diving and engaging the unsuspecting victim. His firing pass hit home, forcing the Tommy to lose altitude. The enemy pilot was nonetheless able to put the stricken aircraft down on its belly, landing on the frozen surface of the Zuiderzee. The five crewmembers were able to evacuate the blazing aircraft [a 15 Sqn Wellington] and were taken captive. Lt. Bockemeyer serving with II./NJG 1 likewise made contact with a Wellington, but was hit in the port engine by the bomber's defensive fire and forced to break off. The enemy bomber was apparently crippled and seen to go down in a steep dive indicating likely another victory. As it subsequently proved impossible to locate the wreckage this victory was not officially recognized. However, moments later Lt. Fellerer (Bordfunker Ogfr. Hätsche) reported a "genuine" victory. In cooperation with a Würzburg ground search radar, he had been excellently vectored onto a "Handley-Page" and shot it down in flames at an altitude of 2,600 meters [a 49 Sqn Hampden]. Our night fighters reported two further engagements with enemy bombers that night but in both cases were unfortunate to return empty-handed. On the other hand, our long-range intruders, the Fernnachtjäger, enjoyed one of their best nights thus far. Oblt. Schulz was the first to score, dispatching a "Bristol Blenheim" at 01:10 over West Raynham aerodrome at just 200 meters altitude. Although Schulz subsequently had to evade the close attentions of a British night fighter, he was able to jettison his ordnance (120 incendiaries) over the airfield at Waybourne and returned home safely. Hptm. Jung (along with his crew Uffz. Scheurks and Gefr. Thomas) was the second intruder to report a victory. At 02:30 he downed a Wellington [of 115 Sqn] in flames, likewise at 200 meters altitude over West Raynham. He too was subsequently able to drop his incendiaries, the resulting fires engulfing Coltishall aerodrome. At around 03:00 he was engaged at 800 meters altitude off Great Yarmouth by a "Blenheim." Accepting combat, he was able to loose off three accurate bursts of fire, setting his adversary alight. However, this victory could not be officially recognized nor added to the night's tally, since the crew had been unable to observe the crash and pinpoint its location. At the controls of his Do 17Z, Lt. Feuerbaum had caught a Wellington that he had encountered in the circuit at Marham. Although he scored hits and set the bomber alight,

> he too was unable to observe it crash. Oblt. Semrau was more fortunate in his Ju 88. After pursuing and firing at a "Blenheim" for some 50 minutes with no evident success, he came across bustling activity over Feltwell aerodrome. Closing in from astern on two "Blenheims" orbiting the field, he shot them both down from the lowest possible altitude [two 21 Sqn Blenheims were indeed lost]. Oblt. Hermann reported a further "double." With his crew of Uffz. Böttner and Gfr. Mardel, Hermann brought down two "Hampden-Hereford" aircraft at low altitude over Waddington. Other aircraft deployed on intruder sorties that night dropped 120 incendiaries and 10 50-kg bombs on airfield installations and factories, returning with reports of effective damage. In another incident, 10 50-kg bombs were released by a Ju 88 over a taxiing British aircraft. Ten minutes later the same "Ju" attacked a Wellington orbiting at 300 meters altitude with its navigation lights on. The outcome of the attack was unfortunately not recorded.

While the two NJG 1 victories were confirmed, I./NJG 2 only downed a single Wellington and two Blenheims over England, the other machines only being damaged.

This I./NJG 2 Ju 88 has been forced to make an emergency landing on its return from a sortie.

With the return of fine weather in March, NJG 1 scored no fewer than 11 victories (although two crews were lost in action), while I./NJG 3, which was reduced to two Staffeln, scored one. I./NJG 2 achieved three confirmed victories over England, but lost three crews, including the highly competent Oblt. Kurt Herrmann. According to a British report, Ju 88 C-4 "R4+CH" had taken off from Gilze-Rijen at 23:00 to carry out a patrol over Lincolnshire. Shortly after crossing the English coast, both engines began misfiring. Herrmann tried to turn back, but one engine stopped, followed by the second. An emergency landing had to be made at Hay Green in Norfolk. The resulting crash left the radio operator trapped in the cockpit, which prevented his comrades from setting fire to the wreckage. When questioned, Herrmann reported seven victories (four Hampdens and three Blenheims) in 25 "war flights" over England. In fact, he was officially credited with nine *Luftsiege* (including several "Herefords"). He claimed that one of his tactics was to attach himself very closely to the aircraft under attack, which prevented British antiaircraft batteries from firing for fear of hitting their own machines.

The Nachtjagd was beginning to gain confidence: on the night of March 13/14, four of the 139 bombers that had set out for Hamburg were shot down. Ofw. Paul Gildner (4./NJG 1) was credited with a double that night, downing a Blenheim and a Wellington, while Oblt. zur Lippe-Weissenfeld (4./NJG 1) was wounded. On March 10, Lt. Reinhold Knacke of 2./NJG 1 was credited with the first Stirling to fall victim to the Nachtjagd. And on the 27th, Oblt. Walter Fenske (3./NJG 1) shot down the first Manchester. Knacke's gunner/radio operator Ofw. Kurt Bundrock described a successful *Dunkelnachtjagd* mission:

> we received instructions over the radio as the ground radar stations attempted to plot the track of the incoming enemy and were given information about his altitude and heading. At that point an interception depended on good eyesight, the lighting conditions, and the actions of the enemy pilot—this was before the advent of onboard search radar. Occasionally all you would see would be the exhaust flames, the huge bomber otherwise all but invisible. Even fitted with flame shields, the bright flames and hot gases coming from the exhausts of the enemy aircraft could on occasion be visible from 100–150 meters away depending on how dark it was. A good sign that the enemy was near was the turbulent wash from the enemy bomber's propellers. When our machine began to shake and lurch, we knew for certain that we were behind him. The pilot would by then have fully charged his forward firing armament, flicked up the gun safety catch and had his finger on the trigger, ready to unleash a salvo from our four machine guns and two cannon at any moment.
>
> "There he is! Three o'clock, 300 meters!" At first all you could see was a slight silhouette in the night sky, and then, as we moved in, a more defined outline. Knacke flew his closing approach, keeping some 50 meters below the RAF bomber as it was easier to discern the shape of it against the sky than the horizon where it blended in. The bomber flew in a rocking motion and by now we could recognize the type of aircraft and would know whether we had to watch out for a tail gunner—which they almost all had—a dorsal gunner or both. This was important for the attack that would then follow. In the meantime the pilot's voice came over the headset: "Short Stirling, *Pauke, Pauke!*—I am attacking!" And the ground control station would reply: "Viktor—roger and good luck!" Knacke now slowly began climbing while moving from the side to position himself underneath the

huge four-engined bomber. The difference in size between the two machines was like that between a small sports car and a furniture van (*Möbelwagen*). Now we followed his maneuvers just 30 meters below him. "I hope his bomb load doesn't go up when you hit him, sir," I said through the throat mike. Knacke replied calmly, "I'm aiming for the port wing." This reassured me because if the bombs went off, then we'd be blown to pieces. The Lt. now pulled the nose of the "Me" up so fast that it looked to me as if we were flying straight ahead and the giant "suitcase" was sinking down in front of us as if we were going to fly straight into it. At the same time a long burst ripped from our machine guns and tore into the left wing between the fuselage and engine, right where the fuel tanks were located. We had gotten dangerously close to the Stirling, forcing Knacke to drop away to the right. Once a short distance away from the Stirling he brought us out of the dive and leveled out. We saw some embers and sparks and a trail of lightly colored smoke, but there were no flames. The Stirling started to dive to evade us, but we followed it down. At the same time the tail gunner opened up on us and the bomb bay doors opened as the pilot jettisoned his bomb load. From a slightly higher altitude Knacke loosed off bursts at the right wing, allowing the bullets to tear into the fuselage. The tail gunner was constantly correcting his aim, and when we fired, he could see us better. We had the advantage of speed though, and we quickly veered from his starboard to port side and went below his line of sight. The Stirling began to burn, and pieces started to come off, swept along by the slipstream. We circled around at a constant altitude and watched as the bomber plunged earthwards. At the point of impact there was an enormous explosion. I made a note of the time, wrote a detailed report of the conditions and based on information from the ground controller I made an estimate as to the wreck's location. Ground control asked if we had seen any parachutes. We replied in the negative.

Ofw. Paul Gildner achieved two "kills" on the night of March 13/14, 1941. Note the emblem on the nose of his Bf 110.

April again saw 11 victories awarded to NJG 1. On the night of 10/11, a Bf 110 from 2./NJG 1 collided with a Hampden. Although the pilot was able to jump clear and was credited with the victory, his radio operator was killed. Two other crews from this Staffel were lost in action. At the beginning of the month, I./NJG 2 received a visit from Field Marshal Erhard Milch, evidence perhaps that the Luftwaffe attached great importance to the *Fernnachtjagd* "intruder" tactic at a time when bomber raids on Germany were intensifying. That month, I./NJG 2 returned 17 confirmed victories. However, many of these *Luftsiege* downed over England were training types, involving only one or two airmen, who were usually only

Despite negative experiences during its use in the Zerstörergeschwader in 1940, the Nachtjagd put into service several Bf 110 D-0s equipped with the so-called *Dackelbauch* (dachshund belly), such as "G9+HR" from 7./NJG 1 (probably a result of the shortage of aircraft). The "belly" tank could not be jettisoned, which rendered the aircraft particularly hazardous to its crews as gasoline vapors accumulated in the belly.

wounded or left unharmed. On April 8/9, Fw. Hans Hahn shot down a Beaufighter from 29 Sqn landing at Wellingore. Its two occupants were again unharmed, the pilot being none other than one F/Lt. Guy Gibson who, in 1943, was to become famous for leading the "Dambusters" unit (617 Sqn). I./NJG 3 was credited with two victories.

In May, NJG 1 lost four aircraft on combat missions but added 22 victories to its tally. On the night of 10/11, the young Eckart-Wilhelm von Bonin (6./NJG 1) scored his first success, downing a Wellington. NJG 3 began to gain experience with four victories. On May 2, Dr.med. Otto Möhlenbeck, the flight surgeon attached to Stab I./NJG 2, noted:

> We have moved to Breda. The facilities at Gilze-Rijen are now only used for night operations. We are staying in a pleasant house whose owners seem to have left for England or Curaçao. Nearby we have the Staka of 4./NJG 2, Oblt. Bohn, and a special guest, Mufti, the anteater mascot of 4. Staffel.

Still operating over England, the Gruppe made 11 claims. Only six could be confirmed (a Spitfire, a Hurricane, an Oxford, a Blenheim, and two Wellingtons). In the early hours of May 8, Fw. Wilhelm Lettenmeier's crew (2./NJG 2) on their 19th *Feindflug* (war flight) over England, were intercepted somewhere over The Wash (off the East Anglian coast). The Do17 Z-10 coded "R4+GK" had been sighted by a 25 Sqn Beaufighter against the brightly moonlit cloud below. After a short dogfight the Dornier went down in flames to crash near Boston. Two crewmen bailed out; the pilot perished at the controls. The two survivors declared that their Staffel had eight crews and two Ju 88s in addition to the usual Do 17 Zs. On the 27th, an event temporarily disrupted the Luftwaffe units still based in the west. The battleship *Bismarck* was being tracked by the Royal Navy and

On the night of May 10/11, 1941, the young Lt. Eckart-Wilhelm von Bonin shot down a 115 Sqn Wellington near Tönning, the first of his many victories.

Fw. Heinz Strüning (I./NJG 2) at the controls of his Ju 88 C.

every available long-range aircraft like those of I./NJG 2 was deployed to locate it. That day, the Ju 88s of I./NJG 2 were deployed on this mission, but Ofw. Sommer was forced to return and crashed his 50-percent-damaged aircraft at Lannion after being targeted near Brest … by a Bf 110! All this energy was spent in vain, as the battleship was sunk on the 27th before many of the aircraft had even been put on alert.

Following numerous Bomber Command raids in June, NJG 1 was able to claim 41 victories and I./NJG 3 a further four. By the end of the month, Hptm. Werner Streib leading I./NJG 1 had achieved 15 victories, Oblt. Walter Fenske (3./NJG 1) had won 12, as had Oblt. Helmut Lent and Reinhold Eckardt of 6./NJG 1. A real "nursery" for aces was emerging.

June was a bloody month for I./NJG 2. Its crews claimed around 20 victories, but only 11 could be identified. And on the night of the 13th/14th, the Gruppe lost no fewer than four

Gilze-Rijen 1941. Ofw. August "Emmes" Hiltrop simulates a maneuver for the benefit of Bordmecaniker (flight engineer) Ofw. Paul Mau, from the crew of Oblt. Gerhard Böhme (3./NJG 2).

crews. Two aircraft were shot down by Beaufighters from 25 Sqn, one crashed into a hill, and the fourth struck the surface of the sea while trying to drop a dinghy to a crew that had ditched.

On the night of June 21/22, Ju 88 C-4 "R4+IH" ("R4+JH"?) of 1./NJG 2 was patrolling over England when it was intercepted and shot down by the Beaufighter of a future ace, New Zealander F/O Michael Herrick of 25 Sqn. Only Fw. Otto Wiese survived.

June 22 was the fateful date of Operation *Barbarossa*, the invasion of the USSR. Despite its importance, this offensive had little direct influence on the development or operations of the Nachtjagd.

On the night of June 25/26, a Whitley was claimed by the Staka of 4./NJG 2, Oblt. Paul Bohn, probably a 99 Sqn Wellington shot down in flames at sea. However, its defensive fire killed the German pilot. Radio operator August Hiltrop wrote a report describing what happened next:

> The crew of Oblt. Bohn, comprising Uffz. Walter Lindner (flight engineer) and Hans Engmann (radio operator), had completed their mission and were returning to their base. Their Ju 88 came under night fighter attack and, in the ensuing combat, Bohn was hit and killed. However, his death was not immediately noticed by his crew and it was not until the aircraft began to behave oddly that it was realized something untoward had occurred. Head and upper body bent forward, Bohn's lifeless body was held in his seat by his straps. It would be impossible to land the aircraft. Lindner did what any good flight engineer should do. He took hold of the stick and stabilized the machine. A tricky maneuver in the tight confines of a Ju 88 cockpit. "Sparker" Engmann immediately reported the situation to the airfield. With the aircraft finally under some sort of control, Lindner switched on the Ju 88's Kurssteuerung "autopilot" and set about extracting Bohn from his seat. This was not an easy task, as Lindner was a big man weighing around 100 kilos, while Bohn was no lightweight either—and, more to the point, was also a dead weight … Finally the two crew men managed to lay out the pilot's body in the lower fuselage *Bodenwanne* "bathtub." Instructions arrived from the ground: bail out of the aircraft to the north of France but, before doing so, jettison the body of the deceased through the hatch while triggering the opening of his parachute. Again, this was not easy, but when the aircraft was able to reach the required 3,000 meters, Bohn's body was successfully ejected before the two aviators jumped without difficulty. It was later learned that the lightened aircraft had crashed—near Milan.

Having steered their Ju 88 back over the mainland and then attached Bohn's body to a chute, the two airmen bailed out successfully and landed near Charleville. However, the body of the deceased Staka was not found. It was not until July 8, 1941 that a farmer from Eclaibes (Maubeuge) discovered Bohn's remains. Both airmen were granted special leave and promoted to Feldwebel. Engmann joined another crew but was killed on the night of September 1/2, 1941. Lindner went to flying school.

On June 13, Oblt. Paul Semrau (3./NJG 2) claimed over England what may have been the first Halifax bomber shot down by the Nachtjagd.

Dornier Do 17 and 215 Night Fighters

When Falck established the first night fighter unit in mid-1940 by the simple expedient of redesignating Gruppen from the Zerstörergeschwader, the preferred aircraft for night-fighting became the Messerschmitt Bf 110 almost by default. However, the Bf 110 did not have the endurance to loiter over RAF airfields. At that time Junkers was working on the first "heavy fighter" variants of their high-performance Ju 88 A bomber—bomb bays became fuel tanks and range was impressive. These first fighter versions were the Ju 88 C-2/C-4. However, such was demand for the Ju 88 through 1940/41 that relatively few of the hundreds being constructed were produced as fighters. At the same time Dornier was also taking a keen interest in "heavy" fighters and proposed and built two "fighter" versions of the standard late-1930s Luftwaffe medium twin-engined Dornier Do 17 bomber. There were so many versions of the Do 17 that Dornier arrived at the "Z" variant even before the outbreak of war.

Powered by two air-cooled Bramo 323 Fafnir engines, the first Do 17 Z, D-ABVD, entered flight testing in 1939 and was capable of 400 kph. This top speed was sufficiently impressive for the type to be considered for the role of "stopgap" night fighter—a handful of Do 17 Z bombers of KG 2 were organized into Nachtjagdketten to undertake nighttime patrols after the first RAF raids over Germany. Dornier subsequently proposed removing the glazed nose from a Do 17 Z-3 and replacing it with the (solid) nose from a Ju 88 C-2/C-4. This conversion resulted in the Z-7 "Kauz I" which featured a nose-mounted armament of three 7.9-mm machine guns and one 2-cm cannon. But the layout was soon found to be unsatisfactory, and an entirely new nose was designed, which increased the armament to four machine guns and two cannon. This version, the Z-10 "Kauz II," was unique in that it mounted the first onboard aid for night-fighting—an infrared "spotlight," the so-called "Spanner Anlage" that was later augmented and then replaced by the first-generation FuG 202 Lichtenstein radar. The "Kauz III" was a conversion of the Do 215, an export version of the Do 17 with more powerful inline DB 601 engines. It is not known with certainty how many Z-7s and Z-10s were produced, possibly as few as eight Z-7s some of which became Z-10s, of which around 11 were built.

The Z-7 first entered service with I./NJG 1 in late June 1940. Given command of the new 1. Nachtjagd-Division, it was Kammhuber—former Geschwaderkommodore of KG 51—who firmly believed that suitably converted bombers such as the Do 17Z and Ju 88, flown by experienced crews, would be ideal for *Fernnachtjagd* missions over the UK. A Dornier 17 Z-7 first saw combat near Eindhoven on June 29, 1940, intercepting an RAF Wellington coned by searchlights. Still assigned to I./ZG 1 (Nachtjagd) and flown by Uffz. Hugo Schwarz, the Dornier sustained damage and later crash-landed near Mönchengladbach. Schwarz and his radio operator, Fw. Gerhard Palm, were both injured while the engineer Fw. Ludwig Born died of his wounds.

In August 1940, the Do 17 Z-7s and Z-10s became part of II./NJG 1. Two Staffeln of II. Gruppe flew the Ju 88 C-2/C-4; only 5. Staffel appears to have operated the Do 17 Z-7/Z-10. For example, during the period June to October 1940, Do 17 Z-7s and Z-10s were only used on 19 nights, flying 22 sorties. Uffz. Vincenz Giessübel—formerly of 2./ KG 2, who had been shot down and taken prisoner over France on May 15, 1940 and then released when Germany invaded France—flew his first intruder mission in a Do 17 Z-10 on November 15/16, 1940; he flew just three more before the end of the year. However, the first recorded successful interception by a Do 17 Z-10 came on the night of September 9, 1940, and was the first success of the war for Fw. Hermann Sommer of 5./NJG 1 ... although his claim was optimistic. He had taken off from Gilze- Rijen in a Do 17 coded "G9+DN" at 21:05 and supposedly shot down a Blenheim in the circuit at RAF Waddington, Lincolnshire, at 23:15. The first confirmed kill by a Z-10 came at 21:25 on October 16, 1940, and was credited to Lt. Ludwig Becker who reported:

This Do 215 B-5 "Kauz III" is equipped with infrared Spanner equipment and FuG 202 radar.

> I was well positioned at the correct altitude of 3,300 m and directed onto the enemy by a series of continual corrections. Suddenly I saw an aircraft in the moonlight about 100 m above and to the left. On moving closer I made it out to be a Vickers Wellington. Slowly I closed in behind and aimed a burst of five to six seconds at the fuselage. The starboard engine caught fire immediately and I pulled my aircraft up. For a while the Englishman flew on, losing height rapidly. The fire died away, but I then saw him spin towards the ground and burst into flames on crashing.

The Wellington was a Czech-flown aircraft from 311 Sqn engaged in an attack on Kiel. P/O Bohumil Landa and three of his crew were killed when the bomber crashed at Oosterwolde in the Netherlands; two airmen were captured. Uffz. Werner Fick, also of 4./NJG 1, claimed to have damaged an unidentified Wellington over the Ijsselmeer inland bay at 00:30 later that night.

Ofw. Paul Gildner of 4./NJG 1 (center, with Ritterkreuz) poses with his crew in front of his Do 215 "G9+NM," the aircraft in which he scored three successes during the night of June 18/19, 1941. There are at least 15 victory markings on the tailfin. Note the first two are day victories—including an RAF Blenheim bomber—achieved with ZG 1 during the *Westfeldzug* campaign in the West. (via Paul Stipdonk)

In February 1941, General Erwin Rommel came to Tripoli to take command of the Deutsche Afrika Korps (DAK). A few aircraft were diverted to the Mediterranean by the Luftwaffe to protect the convoys and ports supplying this expeditionary corps. While the Zerstörer, transport aircraft, and Ju 87s proved indispensable, the dispatch of a night fighter force was more questionable due to the poor quality of the local airfields and the almost total lack of guidance systems. Nevertheless, elements of 1./NJG 3 were detached to Catania, Sicily.

In fact, the Bf 110s were often used to support the aircraft of III/ZG 26, which were very active in Africa/Sicily. From February to May 1941, 1./NJG 3 was based at Catania, where it operated over Malta, losing at least one aircraft on March 16. In May, it moved to Argos in the Peloponnese to take part in the Operation *Merkur* battles over Crete. It then moved on to Benghazi in Libya and, in August, the excellent Derna airfield, where it was under the command of the Fliegerführer Afrika. It had no known successes during this period and, on November 1, it returned to Germany, giving way to I./NJG 2 from the Netherlands.

On November 15, 1941, I./NJG 2 flew south. During the stopover in Munich-Riem, the airmen were vaccinated and given tropical equipment. Then it was off to Sicily. The unit was soon engaged over Africa and Malta, losing two aircraft in bombing raids on the island. Five *Abschüsse* are said to have been achieved against Beaufighters, Blenheims, and Hurricanes.

A Bf 110 of 1./NJG 3 seen here after a belly landing following a sortie over the Mediterranean. The unit retained its largely unsuitable overall black camouflage finish and the "L1+" code.

In Profile:
Ju 88 C NJG 2

Ju 88 C-4 flown by Lt. Hans Hahn of I./NJG 2:

"… We are very proud of our young Ofw. Hans Hahn, recently promoted to Leutnant. He has raced from victory to victory, a skilled proponent of the night attack, but also a master of dealing with the most difficult situations. In the last few months alone, he has completed four single-engined landings, an undertaking that is now banned in favor of belly landings due to the danger it poses to the crew. Hahn has also brought down several barrage balloons, ramming one during an attack. Half the balloon was still wrapped around the stationary engine when he landed. A trophy for our mess! After his last victory he was at the end of his tether and exhausted. He couldn't hide his discomfort. I sent him to Bad Kudowa for rest and it was there that he received the news that he had been awarded the Ritterkreuz." (Dr.med. Otto Möhlenbeck)

Piercing the Darkness: July–December 1941

This period was the eye of the storm for the Nachtjagd. While the force was still being built up much of its new personnel were still in training and operational crews and aircraft were limited in numbers. Despite the best efforts of its creators, it could apparently only engage some 200 aircraft at night. However, this was adequate for the time, as the RAF was unable to launch any sort of major offensive.

German engineers continued to perfect their means of detection. It was around this time that the first Lichtenstein sets were installed in the heavy Dorniers and then in the Bf 110s.

In July, NJG 1 was credited with 35 victories and NJG 3 with four more. It should be noted that the Bf 110s of II./ZG 76 based in the Netherlands occasionally took part in night engagements, winning three victories. Among the successful pilots was Oblt. Wilhelm Herget, who had just returned from the disastrous campaign in Iraq and was soon to make a name for himself at the Nachtjagd. Half a dozen Nachtjagd aircraft were lost in combat that month, one reportedly shot down by a German fighter. Others returned without too much trouble, such as the one flown by the capable Oblt. Helmut Lent (4./NJG 1).

Maintenance on the nose armament of a Bf 110 of NJG 1 at a Dutch airfield.

Nachtabschüsse der 3./N.J.G.2

Hptm.	Hülshoff	20.10.40
Lt.	Hahn	24.10.40
Hptm.	Hülshoff	23.11.40
Oblt.	Bohn	17.12.40
Ofw.	Beier	17.12.40
Lt.	Hahn	2.1.41
Lt.	Böhme	3.1.41
Oblt.	Semrau	11.2.41
Oblt.	Semrau	11.2.41
Lt.	Hahn	12.3.41
Lt.	Hahn	12.3.41
Lt.	Völker	3.4.41
Lt.	Hahn	8.4.41
Lt.	Hahn	9.4.41
Ofw.	Beier	10.4.41
Uffz.	Köster	10.4.41
Lt.	Völker	16.4.41
Lt.	Hahn	16.4.41
Lt.	Hahn	21.4.41
Lt.	Völker	24.4.41
Lt.	Völker	24.4.41
Lt.	Völker	24.4.41
Fw.	Diehne	24.4.41
Lt.	Hahn	3.5.41
Lt.	Hahn	4.5.41
Oblt.	Semrau	7.5.41
Ofw.	Beier	7.5.41
Uffz.	Köster	7.5.41
Uffz.	Köster	8.5.41
Ofw.	Beier	11.5.41
Oblt.	Semrau	12.5.41

Ofw.	Beier	4.6.41
Uffz.	Köster	12.6.41
Oblt.	Semrau	13.6.41
Ofw.	Beier	15.6.41
Ofw.	Bussmann	16.6.41
Ofw.	Bussmann	17.6.41
Oblt.	Semrau	[illegible]
Ofw.	Lüddeke	22.6.41
Ofw.	Beier	6.7.41
Ofw.	Beier	6.7.41
Ofw.	Beier	6.7.41
Ofw.	Beier	6.7.41
Fw.	Barth	7.7.41
Oblt.	Semrau	7.7.41
Fw.	Köster	13.7.41
Fw.	Köster	15.7.41
Ofw.	Bussmann	7.7.41
Oblt.	Semrau	18.7.41
Ofw.	Beier	18.7.41

The victory list of 3./NJG 2 up to July 17, 1941. It is unlikely that all these *Luftsiege* were confirmed.

Fernnachtjagd was awarded 18 victories, but it seems that only eight of these were achieved, the other aircraft only being damaged. Losses were serious. On July 8/9, Ju 88 C-2 "R4+MH" crewed by Lt. Rudolf Stradner (1/NJG 2) did not return to Gilze-Rijen. Flying on one engine (according to the last radio message), it came down off the Dutch coast. On the night of July 21/22, Lt. Heinz Völker was on patrol near Bassingbourn airfield. Fatigue or bad weather prevented this crew from spotting a Wellington of the 11 OTU engaged in the landing phase in time and the two collided in midair, both crews being killed. Völker was officially credited with seven victories (six being certain). Two other crews were lost at the end of the month. On July 23/24, Ogfr. Heinrich Ladiges (4./NJG 2) was reportedly hit by antiaircraft fire over Elsham and, on the night of July 27/28, Lt. Dr. Lothar Bisang (2./NJG 2) was credited with his first and only victory over an Oxford before hitting the ground while trying to lose a Havoc fighter.

On July 9, a youthful Lt. Hans Hahn is awarded the Ritterkreuz.

On July 9, 1941, three Ritterkreuze were awarded for night-fighting: Ofw. Paul Gildner (4./NJG 1) for his 14 victories—on the night of June 18/19, this former ZG 1 pilot had, at the controls of a Do 215, obtained three *Luftsiege* over the North Sea during a raid on Bremen; Lt. Hans Hahn (3./NJG 2) had "only" 11 victories to his name but these were claimed on dangerous intruder missions, and Generalmajor Josef Kammhuber, evidently awarded for his organizational skills, which had enabled the *Himmelbett* system to be set up quickly. He received the honor after the 500th victory credited to 1. Nachtjagddivision.

In Profile:
General der Flieger Josef Kammhuber

Born on August 19, 1898, in Burgkirchen, Bavaria's Josef Kammhuber fought as an infantryman in the Great War before remaining in Weimar's rump army. In 1934, he joined the RLM (the Air Ministry) and, after various stints in Staff positions, was promoted to Kommodore of KG 51 (the Edelweissgeschwader) in March 1940. During Operation *Paula* on June 3, 1940, he was shot down and captured. Freed at the end of the Western Campaign after 27 days' captivity, he was appointed Kommandeur of the new 1. Nachtjagddivision and developed its defense system—the "Kammhuber Line." On July 9, as Generalmajor, he was awarded the Ritterkreuz. On August 1, 1941, he took command of XII. Fliegerkorps, which included Flak units, and was appointed inspector of night fighter operations. Despite his efforts to improve the Reich's air defense, he clashed with Göring when RAF Bomber Command stepped up its attacks in 1942. On November 15, 1943, he was dismissed from his post and spent some time in the reserves before leading Luftflotte 5 in Scandinavia. He again had differences of opinion with his superiors and on October 10, 1944 was posted away, ending the war as commander of jet units. Postwar he became the first Inspector of the new Federal German air force. He died on January 25, 1986, in Munich.

General Kammhuber following his award of the Ritterkreuz.

The upsurge in Bomber Command raids in August, following the continuation of good weather, enabled NJG 1 crews to be credited with around 50 *Abschüsse*. On the night of August 8/9, 1941 some 54 RAF bombers were dispatched to the port of Kiel, while 44 bombed Hamburg. Oblt. Becker claimed a 301 Sqn Wellington, the only aircraft that failed to return from Hamburg, while Lt. Knacke of 2./NJG 1 and his radioman Uffz. Bundrock shot down one of the Kiel raiders, probably a 10 Sqn Whitley. Bringing down a large bomber was no easy matter and the night fighter often had to mount several attacks as Bundrock recorded in his memoir:

> The ground control at the Würzburg-Riese (*Dunkelnachtjagd* area Wolf) on Sylt Island guided us over the North Sea between Sylt and Heligoland onto a twin-engined Whitley. Knacke made his first attack from below and from the side. The only effect was a few defensive maneuvers and a series of tracers from the tail gunner. During the entire dogfight I kept the transmitter button depressed so that ground control could follow what was going on. This way they would be able to send a search team to fish us out of the cold waters as soon as possible. We made our second attack from slightly below and directly behind the enemy. It was unsuccessful. We couldn't get in close enough due to the defensive fire. During the third attack we closed from the rear to take out the gunner from about 80 meters. The Whitley banked into a turn that usually only a fighter plane would make and we knew that a first-rate pilot must be flying her. We heard bullets slamming into our kite during the firefight. We made our fourth pass as the Whitley was doing wild aerobatics and a few shots hit her in the belly which caused some ripping but no flames were visible. During the fifth pass, we didn't even get one shot off, but something tore into our "crate." We had been conducting these maneuvers at between 1,500 and 2,000 meters. We made our sixth attack, again from behind and from below with the tail gunner still shooting at us. The RAF pilot decided to try and escape by diving down to wavetop height. This would prevent us from attacking from below and force us to attack from within range of his tail gunner. Our faster plane didn't help either, since the larger machine was surprisingly agile. This attack failed to produce any visible damage, but the Whitley's evasive maneuvers had slowed it down. One of our rounds must have hit them in the fuselage. We dove in from above under heavy fire. Again, the bomber's fire rattled against our Messerschmitt and one of our engines began to cough. The Englishman began climbing and turned hard on his right wing and almost lost control, but he regained it a moment later and we noticed white smoke coming out of the starboard engine. Knacke remained quiet and with the port engine starting to splutter, made a wide turn to follow the Whitley. The bomber was to our right and was trailing a medium-length banner of white smoke. Knacke turned to follow and the Whitley slowly came into range. The next salvo tore into the area between the fuselage and left engine. The plane flew on like a lethally wounded animal without making any evasive maneuvers. Then we saw a second smoke trail from the right side of the aircraft. The gunners were silent and we had no idea whether they were dead or out of ammunition. The plane plowed on. During the last attack there was no defensive reaction of any kind and Knacke hit the left wing with short burst which set off a flash of bright flames. After a short dive the bomber exploded in a bright cloud of fire. We watched as a cloud of light smoke billowed up from the spot where the bomber had impacted the water. The brave crew went down into the depths of the North Sea.

By now Knacke's Bf 110 was spewing out white smoke from the port engine and the aircraft was losing altitude. The crew turned for home still some 80 km from Sylt. The radio operator requested that naval rescue teams in the area be notified of their predicament. The fighter controller reported that a rescue boat was in the vicinity, the airfield lighting was being illuminated, and firefighters were on standby. Bundrock continued:

> That was when Knacke told me that we were losing power in the starboard engine. Up until that time, I had never considered the possibility that we wouldn't make it back to our airfield. We had flown on one engine before without problems, but what would happen now that the second engine was losing power? What would we do if it seized? Our position was awful. The starboard engine was still losing power and was starting to splutter. We were slowly, but systematically losing altitude. We could still jump if we were above 850 meters and in addition to our life jackets there was a two-man inflatable life raft behind my seat.

Finally, the airfield came into sight and we could make out the runway lights at Westerland. "Maybe we'll be able to make it," I said hopefully. "We have to be prepared for the worst," Knacke replied softly. We were still about 500 meters above the ground and our airspeed was bleeding off perceptibly. The situation was serious.

> "I'll try and start the port engine to give a little bit more power and altitude," stated Knacke as he pressed the starter. The engine coughed, spit out a few flames and gave up in a shudder that vibrated through the whole plane. It had given up the ghost. Altitude: 300 meters. We were slowly approaching the airfield and we could now see the clear outline of the runway. "If we can make it to the runway, I can belly in," said Knacke, and added a moment later, "Bundrock, take a look at this, but move slowly!" I slowly leaned forward and watched as Knacke moved the stick around as though stirring coffee in a cup. "For God's sake, what are you doing?" I cried out. "The stick doesn't work at all. I'm flying with just the elevators and landing flaps," he replied calmly. At that moment he really impressed me. We had made it back to the airfield on one stalling engine. In expectation of the rough landing, I got free of the parachute and stowed it between the radio sets and just as we touched down, I pulled on the emergency canopy release. At that moment there was a loud bang, the noise of an impact, grinding and flying dirt until the plane finally came to a stop. An unpleasant hissing finally broke the incredible silence that followed. Knacke shouted, "Run!" I noticed that the starboard engine was on fire and the flames were getting bigger and brighter and people were running towards us. Cars and fire trucks were speeding in our direction. Knacke jumped out and over the nose, while I headed for the tail and we both ran as fast as we could to get away from the burning plane. It could have exploded at any minute … in the end the firefighters were able to get a layer of foam onto it in the nick of time. With our heads down, we set out on the long walk back to the mess hall. Neither of us said a word.

Knacke and Bundrock's machine was one of only two Bf 110s lost in combat by NJG 1 during August 1941. Over England, I./NJG 2 claimed four *Luftsiege* at the beginning of the month, which cannot be identified. However, they include Ofw Wilhelm Beier's 12th–14th official victories, rewarded with a Ritterkreuz, which was not presented to him until much later. On the night of 12th/13th, two pilots were credited with four clear victories and, up to the end of the month, four others (two of them certain) were awarded to the Gruppe. On the

Aces continued to appear such as Fw. Reinhard Kollak (1./NJG 1) who chalked up his sixth *Abschuss* over Belgium on August 6/7, 1941. He is seen here (left) with his regular radioman Hans Hermann.

night of August 16/17, however, I./NJG 2 lost Lt. Rudolf Pfeiffer's Ju 88 C-2 "R4+HM" (two victories), which went down in the sea with its occupants off the English coast.

On August 30 two pilots were awarded the Ritterkreuz: Oblt. Helmut Lent, Staka of 6./NJG 1, for his 21 victories (including seven day victories in ZG 76); Oblt. Reinhold Eckardt, Adjutant of II./NJG 1 and also a veteran of 2./ZG 76, had 12 *Luftsiege* to his name.

August also saw the move of 1./NJG 1 (Hptm. Heinrich Griese) from Venlo to the Belgian airfield of Saint-Trond (Sint-Truiden). It had become apparent that while night

A Ju 88 of I./NJG 2 parked by the runway is about to be examined by mechanics.

fighters could intercept bombers flying over the north of Belgium (Flanders), the same could not be said for the south of the country (Wallonia). This move meant that virtually all Belgian airspace could be covered.

September was leaner due to the approach of winter. NJG 1 was only able to claim around 20 *Abschüsse* while losing two aircraft in combat. NJG 3 suffered more. Although it scored six victories, it also lost two aircraft in war flights. Engaged on the other side of the Channel, I./NJG 2 increasingly came up against stiff resistance from their RAF counterparts supported by Flak. Four victories were claimed over England—but only two can be identified. This despite heavy losses. On September 1/2, 4./NJG 2 lost the crew of Fw. Walter Kleine after his Ju 88 C-4 "R4+CM" was shot down by a Beaufighter near Winterton (his victor was probably the famous ace John Cunningham, then W/C of 604 Sqn). On September 16, Ofw. Erwin Veil was unable to escape the beam of a searchlight and an attack from an 85 Sqn Boston. The Ju 88 C-4 "R4+NH" went down off Clacton but its three occupants were able to bail out. All wore the Combat Clasp in Silver for 60 war flights or more, making them clear veterans.

On September 1, Luftwaffe officials had to dig deep to establish a II./NJG 3 at Schleswig. 4./ZG 2 had to be withdrawn from the Zerstörer arm to form 4./NJG 3, with the other two Staffeln coming from the Zestörerergänzungsgruppe, a training unit. As early as the end of 1941, the Nachtjagd was experiencing difficulties in obtaining reserves in numbers. On September 29, a Stab/NJG 3 was set up, probably in anticipation of the increase in strength of the Nachtjagdgeschwader 3. Its Kommodore was the Austrian Maj. Johann Schalk, Kommodore of ZG 26. The unit was based at Stade.

A Bf 110 from NJG 1.

A member of the Stab III./NJG 1 sets the agenda for the following day.

A Bf 110 of NJG 3. For a long time, the unit kept the "L1" code it carried when it was part of LG 1.

The Kommodore of the new NJG 3, Maj. Johann Schalk. He was awarded the Ritterkreuz in November 1940 when he flew with ZG 26.

On October 10, 1941, Ofw. Wilhelm Beier was presented with the Ritterkreuz at Gilze-Rijen airfield by General Kammhuber (left) in the presence of Maj. Wolfgang Falck, Kommodore of NJG 1. Only three of the 12 victories claimed by Beier over England could be confirmed.

The Disappearance of Lt. Hans Hahn

According to Bordfunker Ofw August Hiltrop:

> Night operations over England were becoming more and more difficult and dangerous, but we now had to take part in an operation every two days. One evening Ernst Meissler and I joined up with Lt. Hahn, who at 22 was the best night fighter; his impetuosity could not be restrained. He was a specialist in tactics over England and knew every aspect of the British antiaircraft defenses. He could find the enemy at 500 meters. I had no preconceptions about flying with him, although I had no desire to change crews. But my regular pilot, Oblt. Böhme, had become a Warrant Officer and, absorbed by administrative problems, didn't fly much anymore. The three of us discussed that night's mission and then went to our aircraft. Our flight suits and equipment were already on the bus that was going to take us from our billet (the high school in Breda) to Gilze-Rijen. But just as we were about to board, Uffz. Scheidt, Lt. Hahn's regular radioman, who had just come back from leave, said. "I'm back and I want to fly with my crew." I didn't object—that meant I was guaranteed another day. Not that I didn't have the guts, but one always had to dread the hazards of a flight to England. So Scheidt replaced me. However, as I had taken my parachute, he had to take off without one. The bus set off and those who remained waved goodbye to our comrades. From the ops room I watched the Ju 88 of Lt. Hahn, Uffz. Meissler, and Uffz. Scheidt get airborne. It was one of the first aircraft to depart for England that night. A few hours later, radio contact was broken with our comrades. After a long silence from Hahn's crew, we grew increasingly concerned. And long after the aircraft's endurance had been exhausted, we had to come to terms with the fact that they weren't coming home. After about eight days, we learned via Switzerland that their Ju 88 had collided with another aircraft at an airfield in England. This greatly affected us. My comrade's bed remained empty in our room. I was granted special leave for two days and visited Meissler's parents to tell them of their son's death over England. They lived in Gelsenkirchen-Hessler, near my home.

The night of October 12/13 saw the last *Fernnachtjagd Luftsieg* of I./NJG 2—Ofw. Heinz Strüning claimed a Blenheim from 51 OTU at Upwood. Hitler's personal order was to put an end to these long-distance night-fighting operations over England—I./NJG 2 was ordered to the Mediterranean as quickly as possible to support the Afrika Korps and defend Sicily and the sea convoys. Subsequently, most authors have criticized this decision, agreeing with Theo Boiten who wrote that this "move was incomprehensible to the hard-pressed intruder crews themselves and had one far-reaching consequence; henceforth, Bomber Command (and later the USAAF) was able to expand and develop its operational strength, its training and its bases in relative safety without German interference." The question has to be asked though—when and how was the RAF "threatened" by a handful of aircraft mounting sporadic raids, which more often than not destroyed only a few second-line aircraft? As has been said, the *Fernnachtjagd* concept was ambitious but would have required the commitment of at least one Geschwader rather than a single Gruppe of four Staffeln. The German losses were disproportionate to the results, and most of the claims were exaggerated. At a time when NJG 2 and NJG 3 were struggling to make up their numbers, it was inept to allow I./NJG 2 to operate in an almost suicidal manner over Britain, defended with increasing skill by the RAF and by antiaircraft defenses.

At this time *Helle Nachtjagd* was almost completely abandoned. This tactic, adopted in the early days of night-fighting, depended mainly on weather conditions and relied on the reliability of Flak searchlights. Too easily, British bombers could dive into the darkness to evade Nachtjäger attacks. *Helle Nachtjagd* was therefore superseded by the *Dunkelnachtjagd* (or "dark nightfighting"). According to Boiten:

> General Kammhuber realized that *Helle Nachtjagd* was not à satisfactory long-term solution and therefore soon concentrated all his energies in the development of an efficient ground-controlled interception technique based on the use of ground and airborne radar. The equipment necessary for that purpose was produced in the form of the long-range Freya radar, the precision Würzburg Riese with a range of 40 km, the Seeburg Tisch (an accurate plotting table with a radius of 36 km) and the Lichtenstein BC A1 radar which was given industrial priority No. 1 in July 1941.

Gradually, the strategic locations and the Kammhuber Line were divided into 96 *Dunkelnachtjagd* Gebieten, which could be patrolled by two or three fighters alerted to the arrival of enemy bombers. In so doing, the Germans took advantage of the RAF's tactics of the moment: a force of bombers operating over a broad front and not in concentrated streams.

The Nachtjäger were to rely increasingly on the Lichtenstein on board their aircraft. In the last two months of the year, NJG 1 was credited with around 20 victories, which was a lot for a winter period. All this while losing only one aircraft in combat.

But the most significant event at the end of 1941 was the long-awaited increase in the strength of the Nachtjagd. On November 1, NJG 3 was finally complete when, at Stade, II./ZG 76 (the famous "Sharks" Gruppe) became III./NJG 3. Unlike the recently formed II./NJG 3, this was not a unit of novices. II./ZG 76 had fought in the West and over England before operating in Scandinavia. After spending some time in the Mediterranean (a Staffel had fought in Iraq), it had returned to Germany and, as mentioned, had carried out a few night missions in July. II./ZG 76, commanded by Obstlt. Heinz Nacke, included a number of aces such as the veteran Wilhelm Herget and the younger Martin Drewes. Also on November 1, I./NJG 2 left the Netherlands for the Mediterranean. This was an opportunity to create an II./NJG 2 with the existing 4./NJG 2 (which remained attached to I./NJG 2 for a further three months), the former 4./NJG 1 which became 5./NJG 2 and a 6./NJG 2 raised with new personnel. The unit moved to Leeuwarden while a new 4./NJG 1 was reformed with personnel from NJG 1. November 1 also saw the creation of I./NJG 4, about which little is known (see textbox).

During these two months, the brand-new 5./NJG 2 scored 15 victories, most of them by *Experten* from the former 4./NJG 1 (Gildner, zur Lippe-Weissenfeld, Siegfried Ney, etc.).

The list of casualties also mentions many accidents in the Nachtjagd schools. Could this have been the result of extensive training to provide enough crews for all these new units?

A Little-known Gruppe—the "First" I./NJG 4

This Gruppe was apparently established in November 1941, probably in Kitzingen, with Hptm. Walter Spies. It was soon sent to the Eastern Front, but then seems to have merged with the I./ZG 26, with several of its machines bearing the code "3U+." The official victory list strangely mentions only one *Abschuss* of this Gruppe at this time: March 9, 1942, with no name of place or pilot. It is probable that this first I./NJG 4 was "de facto" disbanded around April 1942, when it was led by Hptm. Willi Schurmann. Its crews would then have been distributed to other units, unless they had helped train the small Nachtjagd detachments operating within the Luftflotten engaged in the East.

Lt. Karl Kennel (shown here as Oblt. with Ritterkreuz received in September 1943) is said to have been a member of the mysterious I./NJG 4-I./ZG 26. He was later to join the Schlacht arm.

At the end of 1941, those in charge of the Nachtjagd could draw up a balance sheet. Nine Gruppen flying a mix of Bf 110s, Ju 88s, and Do 215s had been cobbled together with some difficulty, expressly for night-fighting, and very late in the day. One of them was sent to the Mediterranean, while the rest were split between Germany, Belgium, and the Netherlands. One was still in training.

Nachtjagd Gruppen, end 1941

Stab/NJG 1: Deelen

I./NJG 1: Venlo (1./NJG 1 at Saint-Trond)

II./NJG 1: Deelen

III./NJG 1: Twente

Stab/NJG 2: Gilze-Rijen

(I./NJG 2: Catania)

II./NJG 2: Leeuwarden

Stab/NJG 3: Stade

I./NJG 3: Vechta

II./NJG 3: Schleswig

III./NJG 3: Stade

I./NJG 4: Kitzingen

Given the sluggishness with which the NJG 2 and NJG 3 were set up (unlike NJG 1), it appeared that the night fighter arm, despite the efforts of those in charge, was already short of aircraft and personnel, probably because of the growing importance of the Eastern Front and, for some time thereafter, the Mediterranean Front. To obtain a full complement of personnel for NJG 3, it was necessary to absorb a Zerstörer unit (II./ZG 76) which could have been better deployed in the USSR and to transform two training squadrons into combat units. To form II./NJG 2, a Staffel had to be withdrawn from I./NJG 1. By the end of 1941, it was clear that the Nachtjagd had very few reserves.

Another Achilles' heel of the Nachtjagd—which those in charge were probably able to see but were unable to remedy—was the "concentration" of *Experten* or ace pilots. The transfer of Zerstörer pilots to the Nachtjagd had provided the night fighters with competent airmen who were not always experienced in their new, particularly complex task. It was a similar story for the young pilots just out of training. For example, on the night of December 27/28, when two Wellingtons and four Whitleys were shot down, they all fell to aces with impressive records: Ofw. Paul Gildner (22nd and 23rd *Luftsiege*), Hptm. Werner Streib (22nd *Abschuss*), Oblt. Reinhold Knacke (12th victory), Oblt. Heinz-Dieter Frank (6th "kill"), and Oblt. zur Lippe-Weissenfeld (15th victory). This was no accident, but rather proof of the airmanship skills reserved for an "elite" of Nachtjäger. The remaining NJ crews did their best, but the *Experten* were, to coin a phrase, the backbone of the Nachtjagd.

At II./ZG 76 shortly before the transition to III./NJG 3. From left: Oblt. Walter Borchers, Oblt. Hans-Heinrich König, Oblt. Wilhelm Herget, Oblt. Hans-Joachim Jabs, and Obstlt. Heinz Nacke (Kommandeur). Although Jabs and Nacke were already wearing the Ritterkreuz, all five became talented night fighters and received the Ritterkreuz. Only König failed to see out the end of the war.

Hiroshi Oshima, Japanese ambassador and officer, visits III./NJG 3. The aircraft still carry the II./ZG 76 shark's mouth, although they have already adopted the "D5+" code.

Enter "Bomber" Harris: January–June 1942

Organized primarily in the Netherlands from the fall of 1940, German ground and night fighter control defenses were divided into 10 sectors or *Grossräume*. Each of these sectors was 150 km long and 35 km wide. A sector was further subdivided into three sections or "boxes." Each section or *Raum* (lit. room) was equipped with its own combat control post or *Raumgefechtsstand* that, acting on the instructions of the divisional (central) combat command in Zeist (near Utrecht), activated and led defensive actions, tracking incursions with Freya and Würzburg radars. A section usually contained nine searchlight batteries. Night fighters were assigned to an individual "waiting box"—a *Warteraum*—where they would orbit around a Funkfeuer radio beacon awaiting instructions from a fighter controller.

The period up to the end of 1941 was characterized by cooperation with *Abteilungen* (detachments) of Flakscheinwerfer Regiment 1 (AA searchlight batteries) under the command of Ob. Forster, who was also initially in charge of tactical operations. Up until the "dark night-fighting" period there were three *Helle Riegel* ("illuminated defense lines") in the Dutch area. It had been realized that a single "belt" of ground-based radar positions (*Stellungen*) could be bypassed quickly on a narrow front, especially when the bombers were dispatched and flew as part of "stream." This had led to an increase in the "depth" of the radar coverage with sites in front and behind the original *Helle Riegel*, and an upgrading of the sites to enable simultaneous control of two night fighters.

The *Helle Riegel* farthest to the east was the most successful. Operating in the Nachtjagd "boxes" of this third defensive line during the period March–December 1941, Streib's pilots airborne from Venlo accounted for some 24 RAF bombers downed, practicing the *Helle Nachtjagd* procedure (targets illuminated by searchlight); the first of these was a Hampden of 44 Sqn, from Waddington in Lincolnshire, shot down by Streib on March 10, 1941, after an attack on Cologne, and the last, a 57 Sqn Wellington downed by Oblt. Knacke on December 27, 1941.

Both these fighters were directed onto the enemy bombers by instructions transmitted by the ground intercept controller working in what was then Gefechtsstand (command post) 8 C in Meijel (west of Venlo). The instructions radioed to the fighter to complete an intercept took the form of a specific set of codewords, e.g., "Rolf" meant "alter heading 10 degrees to the right," "Lisa" was 10° left. The Meijel control room was led by the highly experienced Jägerleitoffizier (or JLO—ground control intercept officer), Oblt. Walter Knickmeier—fighter controller for Streib's June 11/12, 1943 He 219 sortie.

The difficulties of *Helle Nachtjagd* were self-evident: targets caught in searchlights were often lost again minutes or moments later. Cloud cover was also problematic—if the sky was more than 6/10ths covered, the system was of limited usefulness. And if the target could not be "illuminated," it was extremely difficult to acquire it visually.

As early as 1941, intensive preparations were made to switch over to "guided" or "dark" night-fighting. This planned changeover was linked to the construction of new, more effective night-fighting operations rooms and radar installations. Gefechtsstand Raum 5B in the village of Veulen, 23 km northwest of Venlo, was one of the most important. The three-hectare site had accommodation for some 150 Luftwaffe *Nachrichtenhelferinnen* (female signals auxiliaries) and soldiers, responsible for operating a Seeburgtisch frosted glass plotting table and two Würzburg C radar sets—later supplanted by Würzburg Riesen (Giant Würzburg) radar sets with their seven-meter diameter parabolic dish antenna—in addition to a direct telephone link to the Flugleiter in Venlo, one Hptm. Hitgen, who was in permanent contact with the JLO during the critical takeoff and landing phases of a mission, especially when RAF long-range intruders were being tracked in the vicinity. Each *Raum* had a Freya search radar for longer-range target acquisition, one Würzburg Riese to measure the heading, speed and height of an intruder, the other to track the night fighter. The measured values from both Würzburg radars were transferred to the table—lit up as colored dots—so that "friend" and "foe" were constantly visible to the JLO. The task of the JLO was now to guide the night fighter towards the enemy by setting a "rendezvous point" in such a way that the night fighter could approach the bomber from astern to within visual range, while gradually equalizing its own speed. This was rather more difficult than it sounds—by the time the "returns" arrived in the plotting room to be illuminated on the Seeburg table aircraft travelling at around 100 meters per second were already some distance from their actual location.

Stellung 5B was of particular importance in the initial testing of this guided dark night-fighting procedure. The most experienced crews from Venlo—Streib, Knacke, Meurer, Frank—flew many practice sorties. The first victim to fall to a night fighter controlled by the Seeburgtisch of Gefechtsstand 5B was a Wellington shot down by Knacke on March 13, 1942.

The introduction of a practical airborne intercept radar followed during the spring of 1942. The first onboard aid used by Luftwaffe night fighters was the Spanner, an optical seeker that worked by infrared detection. The first Funkmessgerät (lit. radio measuring device) or radar used on board night fighters was the FuG 202 Lichtenstein BC developed by Telefunken of Berlin. Telefunken opted for a wavelength of 62 cm (490 MHz). The nose-mounted aerial array comprised four fixed double pairs of vertical dipoles on struts with a range of up to around 3.5 km in good conditions, and "provided useful D/F in azimuth and elevation by use of a rotating phase switch which actuated the different antennae in rapid succession." (Green in *Air International*, September 1975). Flight trials of the device had taken place as early as July 1939 but "lethargic" attitudes to nocturnal air defense led to an almost two-year delay before a preproduction Lichtenstein set was available for operational trials in a 4./NJG 1 Do 215 in Holland.

As one Nachtjagd ace Paul Zorner has explained, the device was quite primitive and often unserviceable, especially where aircraft were based near the coast (e.g., Wilhelmshaven) or left uncovered in damp conditions. The "Li-Gerät" as it was known and its improved variants, such as the later SN 2, provided the "fine-tuning" to guide the fighter onto the enemy bomber, once the fighter control officer had pinpointed the RAF machine with the Würzburg and brought the night fighter into the immediate vicinity of the bomber. The Lichtenstein would also facilitate an interception in bad weather or on dark, moonless nights. With onboard radar in the Bf 110, the Bordfunker (BF) was now able to guide his pilot over the last few hundred meters onto the target by directly "measuring" (*das direkte Anmessen*) the enemy aircraft. Ofw. Kurt Bundrock recalled one of his first combat sorties using the Li-Gerät: "the Lichtenstein B/C search radar made finding the enemy much easier. We kept the established hunting areas—*die Nachtjagdräume*—and the JLO on the ground guided us as before in the general direction of the enemy machine. But now when we arrived in the vicinity of the enemy the Li-Gerät would come into play.

"At that point I'd say things like '*Achtung, Ziel erfaßt*—target acquired. *Rechts oben*, up and to the right, 1,900 meters, to the right, more to the right, okay, straight ahead 1,500 meters, slightly up and to the left, more left, more left, 1,300 meters straight ahead, straight, straight, straight, 800 meters, straight, 700 meters, straight, 500 meters.'

"By then and at that point Knacke would confirm that he had visual contact, 'I see him.'

"At that point I would dim the radar screens, we would release the safety of our four machine guns and four cannon, close in to 50–100 meters before opening up with our first burst of fire. If we didn't knock him down with our first salvoes and the bomber was thrown into an evasive maneuver to get away from us, I could usually pick it up again on the radar."

Bf 110 C/D of 4./NJG 1 fitted with the Lichtenstein BC air intercept radar. The aircraft is jacked up for weapons harmonisation. The large "N" on the engine cowl indicated the improved DB 601 powerplant using "C-3" synthetic 100 octane fuel for increased power output. Leeuwarden, Holland, spring 1942.

As more and more night fighters were equipped with Lichtenstein, searchlights gradually became redundant, and these were removed from the *Helle Nachtjagd* sites. However, Lichtenstein had only a limited "pickup" range, which made accurate ground control intercept plotting with the Seeburg table crucial to the procedure. The fact that the instructions between the ground controllers and the NJG crews were transmitted in "plain language" and were being recorded by monitoring stations in England soon led the RAF to work out what was happening.

Also introduced during 1942 was the so-called Y-Verfahren (Jagd) system which enabled ground control of a formation of fighters through radio range-finding (measurement by the HANS E-Mess Gerät) and bearing detection (established by the HEINRICH direction-finding Peiler). Y-Verfahren (Nachtjagd) was soon introduced and would become particularly useful in guiding inexperienced fighter crews towards the incoming bomber stream.

All these various procedures had shortcomings. One of the most striking was the enormous cost and the huge manpower resources invested in dozens and dozens of *Raum* command posts. More importantly the RAF realized that a large number of raiders could pass through the defensive lines with little chance of being intercepted by flying in close formation, i.e., in a "stream"—each "box" could only deal with one bomber at a time.

January 1942 saw an important move when 1./NJG 1 returned to Venlo and II./NJG 1 left Deelen to replace it at Saint-Trond. Thus were born the "infamous" if not to say, feared, "Ghosts of Saint-Trond" (see textbox).

During its time in Saint-Trond, 1./NJG 1 lost Lt. Hans-Joachim Redlich, killed at Meeuwen-Gruitrode during the night of January 11/12, 1942 on a training exercise. Gruppenkommandeur Hptm. Werner Streib is seen at the funeral in Brustem.

In Profile:

Walter Ehle, Kommandeur of II./NJG 1

In January 1942, II./NJG 1 moved into Saint-Trond, led by Hptm. Walter Ehle. Born on April 28, 1913, in Windhoek in the German colony of South West Africa, he joined the brand-new Luftwaffe after graduating in 1935 and trained as a pilot. In 1938, he went to Spain to serve in the fighter unit of the Condor Legion. On his return home, he was posted to ZG 1 and fought in Poland, Scandinavia, and then in the West during *Fall Gelb*. In June 1940, his unit was transferred to the Nachtjagd, with Ehle leading the new 3./NJG 1. On the night of July 20/21, 1940, he claimed his first victory from Münchengladbach, the third official *Luftsieg* of the fledgling Nachtjagd. On October 7, 1940, Ehle was promoted to head up II./NJG 1, and went on to win 26 of his 34 victories from Saint-Trond, receiving the Ritterkreuz on August 29, 1943. On the night of November 17/18, 1943, Ehle returned from Germany in particularly foul weather. On coming in to land at Saint-Trond, the aerodrome lights were extinguished unexpectedly. Disorientated, and probably tired, Ehle hit the ground at Horpmaal. He was buried with his two crew in Brustem, then after the war in Lommel.

Saint-Trond, January 1942. Hptm. Walter Ehle, Gruppenkommandeur of II./NJG 1, returns from a sortie.

Throughout January, 16 victories were achieved by the Nachtjagd, none of which was attributed to NJG 1—14 were claimed by NJG 2 and the other two by NJG 3. On the night of January 15/16, Uffz. Kurt Zipperlein (6./NJG 2) shot down a Whitley from 51 Sqn near Rottevalle. Six days later, on the 21st, Zipperlein himself was shot down in combat off the Dutch coast. He was one of the many "stars" of the Nachtjagd that are unknown. On the other hand, on the same night of January 20/21, his Staka, Oblt. Ludwig Becker, was credited with three Wellingtons (9th–11th "kills") shot down near Terscheling.

The Staka of 6./NJG 2, Oblt. Ludwig Becker, was credited with three Wellingtons on the night of January 20/21, 1942. A former glider pilot, then bomber and Bf 110 pilot with ZG 1, Becker scored his first victory using the Lichtenstein device, which he quickly came to appreciate. He scored 44 night *Abschüsse* and won the Ritterkreuz, but was killed on March 26, 1943, the same day he was awarded the Eichenlaub.

February 1942 was a pivotal month for the Nachtjagd. On February 27, a commando raid led to the capture of a Würzburg radar at Bruneval, a windfall for British specialists. A new CO of Bomber Command had been appointed—Air Marshal Arthur Harris. Harris deplored the poor results and inaccuracy of his bombers' attacks. In the weeks that followed, the RAF was able to develop jamming systems for German detection equipment, as well as improving and better arming its bombers. Above all, Harris was to launch a series of huge "campaigns." In February 1942, German night fighters could only field some 367 aircraft, just over half of which were immediately available at all times. They were divided into three Jagddivisionen which were still poorly equipped, each comprising only one Geschwader when two were planned.

Jagddivisionen, February 1942

I. Jagddivision (Belgium, Netherlands, Ruhr) : NJG 1.

II. Jagddivision (North and North-West Germany, Berlin): NJG 3.

III. Jagddivision (South-West Germany): II./NJG 2.

Taking advantage of this lack of manpower, Harris's tactic was "saturation" despite the very probable losses—the end justifying the means. In February, 10 victories were achieved by night fighters, including the 30th by Hptm. Helmut Lent, Kommandeur of II./NJG 2, which he had been leading since November 1941.

On February 4, 1942, Kommandeur Helmut Lent (II./NJG 2) scored his 30th victory.

For 10 days in February, detachments of NJG 1 were sent to coastal airfields in the Netherlands, northern Germany, and Scandinavia to take part in a special operation: the day and night escort of the *Scharnhorst* and *Prinz Eugen* during the famous *Kanal Durchbruch* (the "Channel Dash," Operation *Donnerkeil*) from Brest. Several Bf 110s were damaged, including the machine flown by Oblt. Herget, who force-landed in Lister Bay after engine failure.

In March, no fewer than 40 victories were scored by the Nachtjagd, which proved its worth despite its limited number of aircraft. However, there were still some familiar names: Oblt. zur Lippe-Weissenfeld (5./NJG 2), who returned four *Luftsiege* on the night of the 26th/27th (18th–21st "kills"); Oblt. Reinhold Knacke (2./NJG 1) who reached 16 victories at the end of March; for Helmut Lent, it was 34 and for Oblt. Reinhold Eckardt (7./NJG 3) 15.

However, fresh, young "daredevils" were beginning to appear. On the night of March 26/27, Oblt. Siegfried Wandam (3./NJG 1) was credited with his second victory, as was Fw. Richard Launer (2./NJG 1). Oblt. Herbert Lütje (Stab III./NJG 1), a future Ritterkreuzträger, returned his fourth victory. And so on. On the other hand, seven Nachtjäger were lost in combat, victims of enemy fire or accidents during combat flights.

During this month, two major raids were launched by the RAF with 235 bombers sent to the Renault factories at Boulogne-Billancourt (March 3/4) while 211 aircraft hit Essen (March 8/9). During this second raid, only four aircraft fell victim to the Nachtjagd. The saturation tactic therefore seemed to be having an effect, even though night-fighting had not been used for Billancourt.

A Lichtenstein-equipped Bf 110.

On the night of March 25/26, 1942, Lt. Johannes Cenkier of 4./NJG 1 took off from Saint-Trond in his Bf 110 "G9+IM" to counter a formation targeting Essen. At Purnode, near Namur, his aircraft suffered an engine failure and Cenkier was killed along with his crewman—one of the seven night fighters lost that month, and a crew that did not have time to prove itself.

A Bf 110 on standby.

In Profile:
Wilhelm Herget

Born in Stuttgart on June 30, 1910, Wilhelm Herget came from a family of printers. A keen aviation enthusiast, he obtained his civilian licence in 1936 and was trained as a fighter pilot during his military service. In 1939, he was posted to 6./ZG 76 (the "Sharks") and fought in the West in Bf 110s, being credited with 14 victories over France and England. He took part in the infamous—and short-lived—Iraq campaign in May 1941. Appointed Staka of 7./NJG 3 and then of 4./NJG 1, he scored his first night victory flying out of Saint-Trond on the night of April 5/6, 1942. Very small in stature, nicknamed "*der Kleine*" ("Titch"), Herget had his mechanic add wooden wedges to the rudder pedals of his aircraft so that he could reach them more comfortably. Herget soon added to his list of achievements and was promoted to command II./NJG 4 on May 1, 1942. On October 1, 1942, he led the new I./NJG 4 operating out Florennes. On June 20, 1943, Hptm. Herget was awarded the Ritterkreuz for his 31 victories. On April 11, 1944, he was awarded the Eichenlaub, bringing his total number of victories to 63. At the end of 1944, he was attached for a time to the General der Jagdflieger's Stab before flying the Me 262 in JV 44. He scored his 73rd and last victory on April 27, 1945, downing a P-47 but was shot down and captured days later, on May 2, while flying an Fi 156 Storch. After the war, Wilhelm Herget returned to Stuttgart and took up his printing trade again. He died in his hometown on March 27, 1974.

Three II./NJG 1 aces seen in Saint-Trond. From left to right: Hans Autenrieth, Eckart-Wilhelm von Bonin, and Wilhelm Herget. All three would survive the war, two of them being awarded the Ritterkreuz.

In front of his comrades at Saint-Trond, Oblt. Hubert Rauh (4./NJG 1) describes one of his dogfights. He was the first Nachtjagd ace to shoot down a British bomber over France at night.

In March, a Stab III./NJG 2 and a 7./NJG 2 were established at Gilze-Rijen. However, lack of manpower meant that an 8th Staffel had to wait until May, and a 9th until June. These three Staffeln had been formed with fresh personnel out of flight schools. Command of this III./NJG 2 was handed to Hptm. Herbert Bönsch. He had led (Z)/KG 30 in 1940 before moving on to NJG 1 and 2.

RAF bombers had learned to avoid the frontal attacks of the Nachtjäger by flying slightly around the Kammhuber Line, which was still under construction. This meant flying over northern France. In April, the first Nachtjagdstaffel to be based in France flew into Laon-Athies: 7./NJG 3 led by Oblt. Reinhold Eckardt. The Staffel was to intercept intruders flying over the Aisne and Ardennes regions while making incursions into southern Belgium if necessary. Naturally, there was some interference in this border region. On April 27/28, Oblt. Eckardt claimed three victories over Belgium, while Oblt. Hubert Rauh of 4./NJG 1 based at Saint-Trond scored his first victory downing a Wellington near Givet, the first bomber to fall victim to the Nachtjagd in France. That same night, II./NJG 1 shot down two Wellingtons of 27 OTU over Belgium on a *Nickel* mission (dropping leaflets) in the Lille sector.

Rauh's victim, a Wellington (from 304 or 300 Sqn) that came down near Givet on April 27/28, 1942.

Oblt. zur Lippe receiving his Ritterkreuz from General Kammhuber.

In Profile:
Bf 110 D NJG 2

Messerschmitt Bf 110 D-3 flown by Oblt. Rudolf Sigmund of the Stab II./NJG 2, September 1942. Appointed Staka of 10./NJG 1 on October 1, 1942 Sigmund had achieved eight *Nachtabschüsse* by this stage of his career and would take his total to 28. The camouflage finish is an overspray of RLM 74/75. Note the green spinners of the Gruppenstab and the small FuG 202 Lichtenstein array.

A new Nachtjagd Gruppe, II./NJG 4 (code "3C"), was set up at Laupheim. Once again, it was a very makeshift operation, as 5./NJG 4 was the former 5./ZG 26, the other two Staffeln being formed with new personnel. The new Kommandeur was Hptm. Wilhelm Herget. The following month, II./NJG 4 moved to Rheine.

In April, the Nachtjagd was credited with 64 victories, a high figure explained by the new tactics introduced and imposed by Air Marshal Harris, but also by the increase in the number of night fighter units. All the NJ Geschwader were involved: NJG 1, 2, 3, and 4. German losses were half a dozen fighters shot down.

On April 16, Oblt. Egmont Prinz zur Lippe-Weissenfeld (5./NJG 2) was awarded the Ritterkreuz for his 21 victories. The previous year, a dozen would have been largely sufficient to qualify for the award.

In May, the Nachtjagd was augmented by a III./NJG 4 created at Mainz-Finthen with personnel from the 1, 4, and 8./NJG 1. Its Kommandeur was Maj. Kurt Holler, ex-Staka of the 1. and 9./NJG 1, who had no victories to his name but was appointed to the post because of his organizational skills.

It goes without saying that night fighter crews sometimes had to take risks to score. On the night of May 19/20, near Brustem, Oblt. Fritz Gutezeit, Staka of 6./NJG 1, got too close

The wreckage of a 7 Sqn Stirling and Oblt. Gutezeit's Bf 110 following their collision.

to his target and his Bf 110 E-1 collided with a 7 Sqn Stirling in midair (his second and last victory). Both aircraft crashed to the ground with their crews.

But the month of May was marked by the night of May 30/31 and the first of the so-called "thousand bomber raids" conceived by "Bomber" Harris to deal the Nachtjagd a crushing blow by dispatching the bombers—over 1,000—in a continuous compact stream against a large city, in this case Cologne. Only by committing virtually the entire frontline strength of his bomber command could Harris assemble the hundreds of aircraft sent on the raid, using training aircraft from the OTUs where necessary. The tactic was a success and, as expected, the *Dunkelnachtjagd* defenses were overwhelmed by the mass of 1,046 bombers spread over 30 kilometers—only a proportion of the 43 losses were attributed to the Nachtjagd. Despite good "hunting" conditions (full moon), losses were reduced because of the "concentrated stream." Nonetheless, some 30 bombers fell victim to NJG 1 and 2, with a further 12 aircraft returning with damage attributable to the fighters. This was almost half of the Nachtjagd's victories for the month—on the last night of the month. Most of the losses occurred on the return leg when the formations had spread out, which favored *Dunkelnachtjagd*—the night fighters did not lose a single crew. A double victor that night was Lt. Helmut Niklas of 6./NJG 1 (see textbox).

Funeral ceremony at Brustem for Gutezeit and his crew.

In Profile:
Helmut Niklas

Born on August 8, 1920 in Munich, Lt. Niklas flew in 6./NJG 1. On the night of May 30/31, 1942, he scored his first two victories, as described by his radioman, Uffz. (Heinrich?) Wenning:

> We did not patrol our zone for long because, at an altitude of 3,000 meters, we encountered our first victim, some 400 m away. At virtually the same time, the Tommy spotted us. He turned sharply to the right and swooped down. We pursued him but his fire was so intense that we couldn't adjust and overtook him. Lt. Niklas made such a sharp turn that my navigation equipment scattered all over the cockpit floor. We dropped back behind the bomber and, at close range, sprayed shells into its left wing. It caught fire and flames leapt from the wing. By this time the Wellington had dropped to 1,800 m. We fired another salvo into the fuselage and wings and the fire spread. We kept our distance to check whether a second pass would be necessary. The Wellington continued to fly for a short time as the fire grew. It then slipped over on its wing and plunged towards the ground, trailing a plume of flames like a comet. It exploded close to the ground, lighting up the surrounding countryside. A feeling of satisfaction washed over us: this was our first victory. I pounded my pilot's shoulders with both fists ... We descended to 180 m to view the crash site. The base quickly sent us a bearing so that we could determine our position and then guided us to another prey ... I was suffering from a lack of oxygen because we were flying at 5,000 m without a mask. I was then surprised to see a Tommy ahead of us at 600 m distance. It was another Wellington. It zigzagged but didn't open fire. We launched the attack. The target grew and suddenly seemed enormous. Were we going to ram him? We opened up at close range and hit it in the wings and fuselage. We saw glimmers of impacts in

Lt. Niklas (6./NJG 1) belly-landed his machine at Saint-Trond on the night of May 30/31, 1942 (the first RAF "thousand-bomber raid") having claimed two victories.

> the rear fuselage. I was about to say, "It's on fire," when suddenly Lt. Niklas shouted, "I've been hit, I'm breaking off." I had mistaken the glow of the enemy machine-gun fire for the impact of our projectiles.

Niklas had been hit in the left arm and Wenning put a tourniquet on it with a piece of string he had in his pocket. The Wellington's return fire had destroyed part of the instrument panel, including the compass but the two men flew on. Near Saint-Trond they asked for the runway to be illuminated, but this was refused because of the presence of "*Kurier*" (enemy aircraft) in the area. Finally, considering the desperate situation—they could not bail out—the runway lights were quickly flashed on and Niklas, on the verge of passing out, guided by his "sparker," landed the aircraft on its belly. He hit his head on the dashboard and Wenning had to extract him from the cockpit and drag him to the ambulance that arrived on the scene. The first Wellington had crashed at Montigny-le-Tilleul, while the second was found south of Landen.

Niklas most likely left II./NJG 1 after this episode, but was promoted to Oblt. and became Staka of 6./NJG 3. The following year, he added three bombers to his scoreboard, all shot down over Germany, one of them a B-24 encountered during a daylight mission on October 8, 1943. In December 1943, Niklas took command of 2./NJG 3, but on January 30, 1944, during another daylight engagement, he was killed at Alten-Rheine.

Lt. Helmut Niklas and his mascots.

In addition to these 30 claims, the Nachtjagd was said to have shot down 27 aircraft between May 1–29. Keen to keep up the pressure on the Nachtjagd and Flak, Harris immediately launched a second thousand-bomber raid on the night of June 1/2, this time on Essen. In the event "only" 956 bombers were assembled, 31 of which were lost; 21 were attributed to the Nachtjagd. Given the dense cloud cover, this raid was considered a failure.

It was on this night that Heinz Schnaufer returned the first of his "record" 121 nighttime *Abschüsse*. His Bordfunker Fritz Rumpelhardt recalled events in his diary:

> On June 1, 1942, I received the news that I had been made up to the rank of Uffz. I had barely sewn my new shoulder boards on, when we were ordered up on our 13th combat sortie. We took off at 01:04 to patrol in Raum 6C. Weather conditions were ideal. We experienced no difficulty raising the fighter controller who came over loud and clear on the frequency and, all things considered, conditions were ideal. We had been airborne for some 40 minutes when our controller vectored us onto a target flying homeward at 3,500 meters altitude. We were guided in until we received the obligatory "targets have contact" which meant that the two Seeburg traces representing our fighter and the bomber had merged on the operator's table. Despite this, we had to yet to make visual contact with the target. After several course corrections in liaison with the ground station I thought that I had sighted a barely perceptible darker shadow above us on the starboard quarter against the horizon. I immediately directed Schnaufer towards it and after a few moments we clearly recognized the bulk of an enemy aircraft—a Halifax. We eased out some 150 meters to the side. Now it was a question of calming the nerves since the bomber had shown no signs of having spotted us as it doggedly plowed on through the night skies.
>
> Up to now we had exchanged the bare minimum of words. I marveled at Schnaufer's calm and composure. The only thing that counted at this moment was the imminent attack. The theory had been rehearsed and these very scenarios ran through his mind hundreds of times. He would pull up the nose of the fighter, flip up the "spoon"—the armament selection cover switch on the head of the control column enabling the pilot to coordinate flight maneuvers and weapons firing—depress the gun-firing button with the aid of the "spoon" and let the bomber fly through the burst of fire. In the last seconds of the maneuver the pilot would then throw the stick forward and to the side, peeling away to get clear of the tail gunner's or ventral gunner's potential radius of fire. This was in fact the Achilles' heel of this tactic since under these conditions the night fighter made an ideal target for the tail gunner's four machine guns. So much for the theory, though. I reported to the fighter controller that we were making "*Pauke Pauke*," the codeword for an attack and then all hell broke loose.
>
> Our first burst raked the bomber's wing, setting it ablaze, while a huge sheet of flame erupted on our second, which was sufficient to decide the fate of the huge bird. At no time did we observe any defensive fire. We eased out to one side, clearly able to see the RAF roundels by the light of the tongues of flame and looked on as the crew took to their parachutes, happy enough that they were alive and heading into captivity. Our joy at our first victory was boundless. A long and barely intelligible howl of pleasure resonated through the ether to the ground station where the celebrations were barely any less restrained. The success was as much theirs as it was ours. Suddenly the Halifax slipped down over one wing

> and plunged earthwards. The impact, 15 km south of Leuven, Belgium, and the ensuing detonations could be seen for miles around.

Loading new magazines in the heavy MG FF cannon, Rumpelhardt was directed onto a new contact at around 03:00. Schnaufer had the throttle "against the stops" as they slowly came in behind another "Tommy" and by the time "targets have contact" had been reported they found themselves in Raum Gent, barely able to make out the instructions of the ground controller. They continued with their westerly heading until Rumpelhardt managed to discern a slightly darker form ahead and off to the side. Initially unable to agree on the aircraft type, they agreed that this was another four-engined machine and therefore "belonged on the other side of the sewer." Rumpelhardt:

> At around 390–400 kph the relatively high speed of the enemy aircraft rather surprised us. Schnaufer once again positioned himself some distance underneath the target. After a spell of observing our prey Schnaufer carried out his first attack aiming for the starboard wing. There were no visible results. After unleashing a second salvo a small flame could just about be discerned. The high speed of the Tommy meant that we couldn't press home the attack on the third firing pass. As a result, we were getting in close and thought we could make out hits in the wing, all the more since we were flying through a plume of vaporized fuel streaming back out of his wing tank. With all barrels blazing we closed to within 20 meters. This audacity was to prove to be our undoing since heavy machine-gun fire hammered against our fighter. Banking the "Me" sharply over, we broke off and peeled away.
>
> After leveling off, we were able to assess the effects of the defensive fire. The pilot had taken a bullet in his left leg. Our port engine appeared to be on fire

Fritz Rumpelhardt, on a visit to his wounded "*Kutscher*" (lit. coach driver, i.e., pilot), brings Schnaufer a piece of the roundel of the Halifax of 75 Sqn shot down at Grez-Doiceau on the night of June 1/2, 1942.

and had to be shut down. One of the rudders was inoperable, the control cables almost certainly having been shot through. Our landing light was on and couldn't be extinguished, leaving us lurching around like an illuminated target. We were so preoccupied with our own straitened circumstances that we couldn't observe the effects of our last pass. We were in something of a quandary to say the least. The first thought was to bail out. However, this wasn't exactly advisable at 600 meters altitude. Fortunately, we were able to restart the engine that had been stopped and once again climb for altitude. However, we had now been airborne for some considerable time and there was not much left in the tanks. We decided to head for home. Given the distance we were from the controller in Raum 6C, establishing communication proved fruitless. Having managed to contact the field at Saint-Trond, I managed to take a QDM radial with the trailing aerial. I had to fire off two recognition flares and one red distress signal before the runway lighting was finally switched on for us.

The landing approach was a little tricky since with one rudder knocked out, turns could only be flown with the ailerons, in other words in an extremely steep bank. Following touchdown it was as much as the pilot could do to keep the machine on the tarmac. It suddenly veered off to the left and we were in crash area, the field adjacent to the runway. Ignition off and stamp on the brakes until they were red hot! The crate finally came to a stand and suddenly there was unbelievable quiet and stillness all around us. We had certainly never been so happy to clamber down from the "Me" as now. As we had come in on final approach, I had radioed that we required medical assistance. We now immediately loaded the pilot into the ambulance and he was driven off to the sick bay. Our "Dora-Cäsar" had taken about 19 hits all told. I think I was the only part of the crate that wasn't hit. In the end though our patience had paid off. We no longer had any need to fear comparison with the other successful crews.

Kommandeur Walter Ehle poses in front of his tailfin displaying nine victory bars (the ninth being a Wellington shot down on the night of June 1/2, 1942). There were two victories over Polish aircraft in September 1939, a Spitfire at Dunkirk and six bars with diagonal black stripes symbolizing successes achieved at night. The Spanish Cross, an award from his time with the Condor Legion, is pinned to his jacket.

In Profile: Bf 110 NJG 1 & NJG 4

Oblt. Gustav Uellenbeck of the Stab II./NJG 1, Deelen, Holland, May 1941. On May 9, 1941, Lt. Uellenbeck crash-landed this Bf 110, "G9+BC," after being shot down by German Flak. A former ZG 76 pilot, he had claimed two victories during the Heligoland Bight air battle of December 18, 1939. He died on August 14, 1941 from injuries sustained after hitting the ground during a night sortie on August 3, 1941. His Bordfunker, Uffz. Alfred Sprenger, was also killed.

Bf 110 F of 7./NJG 4, flown by Stabsfeldwebel Reinhard Kollak of 7./NJG 4. Upon completion of his fighter pilot training in the spring of 1940, Kollak was posted to I./ZG 1 and participated in the campaigns in France and the Battle of Britain. In October 1940 Kollak was posted to the newly formed 1./NJG 1 and claimed his first night victory while flying as a Feldwebel with I./NJG 1, shooting down a Whitley in the early hours of June 17, 1941. He remained with I./NJG 1 when it was redesignated 7./NJG 4 in May 1942, and on the night of August 24/25, 1942, shot down a Stirling, his 10th *Abschuss*. The F-subtype was the first dedicated night-fighter variant of the Messerschmitt Bf 110. The aircraft is equipped with the FuG 202 B/C Lichtenstein AI radar Gerät. Kollak was the highest-scoring NCO Nachtjagd pilot and the most successful pilot in III./NJG 4. He was awarded the German Cross in Gold on April 12, 1943, precursor to the Ritterkreuz which followed in early 1944 with his "score" at 29 victories. He achieved an *Abschusszahl* of 49 victories and flew over 250 sorties but never received higher decorations because of his NCO status. His BF Hans Hermann joined the Luftwaffe in 1938 and flew with Kollak until the end of the war.

Admitted to hospital in Brussels, Schnaufer did not fly for another month.

Between June 2 and 24, the Nachtjagd scored 74 victories. Then came the night of June 25/26, the third thousand-bomber raid, against Bremen: 44 bombers were lost, 36 of them to night fighters.

Another 15 *Luftsiege* were gained in the last two raids of the month.

Overall, in June, the Nachtjagd returned 146 victories, a record since its establishment. But it had lost at least 16 aircraft in combat, most of them with their crews. These were heavy losses. Night engagements were now turning into a war of attrition. Some writers have questioned the importance of these three thousand-bomber raids, which they claim alerted the Nachtjagd prematurely to its weaknesses. One of the most glaring was its lack of reserves. But how could those in charge have remedied this in such a short space of time? On June 6, Hptm. Helmut Lent, Kommandeur II./NJG 2, was awarded the Eichenlaub for his 42 victories.

On June 30, faced with increasingly deadly Bomber Command raids, Hitler ordered all searchlights to be reassigned to the Flak arm protecting German cities. As a result, a large number of Scheinwerfer units assigned to the Kammhuber Line in the Netherlands, Belgium and France were moved back to cover German cities and strategic industrial sites. This marked the end of the *Helle Nachtjagd*, which had gradually become obsolete as crews increasingly relied on the Würzburg, Freya, and Lichtenstein rigs.

Still operating in the Mediterranean, I./NJG 2 was now led by Kommandeur Erich Jung. The unit had four Staffeln, which would split up regularly, moving to Athens, Derna, or Benghazi as and when required (reconnaissance, convoy escort, etc.). I./NJG 2, like most German units operating from Sicily, were *Mädchen für alles* ("jacks of all trades") who would search for enemy aircraft on Malta and, if necessary, drop a few bombs on the island. This was due to the weakness of the Luftwaffe in this theater.

May 1942. At Kastelli, Kommandeur Erich Jung talks to Lt. Georg Wiedow, the Gruppe adjutant. Wiedow and his crew were killed by a Beaufighter near El Alamein on July 6, 1942.

As early as January 8, one crew did not return from Malta, likely a victim of AA. Three victories were claimed that month, but another Ju 88 C-2 crashed in Sicily, probably damaged in combat. Three victories and a sole loss were reported in February, and even the destruction of a submarine was claimed, which must be doubtful. March saw three more losses, including one in Africa.

In April, the unit received Ju 88 C-6s with more powerful engines and superior armament to the C-2. That month, the I./NJG 2 lost two crews but claimed two victories over Africa. In May, a Staffel was able to operate from Kastelli airfield in Crete. Three victories were achieved but one crew was killed near Bardia.

June was more eventful, with 10 victories, including three by Lt. Heinz Rökker (1./NJG 2). Rökker returned on June 20 and 29 with a damaged aircraft and was himself wounded along with his regular observer, Fw. Carlos Nugent. A Ju 88 C-2 was lost with its crew in Africa, while several other twin-engined aircraft were damaged.

A Ju 88 "Cäsar" at Kastelli (Crete).

Luftsiege Mount: July–December 1942

Whereas prior to Harris's arrival at the head of Bomber Command, bomber attacks had involved between 50 and 100 aircraft, the Luftwaffe now had to confront regular incursions by anything up to 300 aircraft. Not surprisingly, the Nachtjagd scored 101 victories in July.

At the end of that month, Hptm. Werner Streib (Stab I./NJG 1) had 32 victories to his name, Oblt. Reinhold Knacke (I./NJG 1) 28, Oblt. zu Sayn-Wittgenstein (9./NJG 2) 17, etc. On the night of July 28/29, Knacke became the first Luftwaffe night fighter ace to shoot down a Mosquito (a 23 Sqn machine DD 677) over the Netherlands. In his memoir Knacke's BF Kurt Bundrock recalled that he did not even know what a Mosquito was at that time, while Knacke assured his BF that it was only the second Mosquito shot down—ever: "I went out to crash site this morning. The thing is constructed entirely of wood and tremendously fast as a result. I'm telling you, it can manage 600 kph." De Havilland's fast twin would virtually revolutionize the night air war and with its unrivaled performance would prove to be a real headache for the night fighter aces right to the end of the conflict.

Ten Nachtjäger were lost in action during July 1942. The most serious loss was that of the Staka of 7./NJG 3, Oblt. Reinhold Eckardt, killed during the night of July 29/30. Having taken off from northern France to intercept a formation of 275 bombers heading for Saarbrücken, he scored his last three victories over Belgium for his 23rd–25th *Abschüsse* (a 149 Sqn Stirling timed at 01:15, a 419 Sqn Halifax at 02:51, and a 50 Sqn Lancaster at 03:06). However, while closing on a fourth enemy aircraft near Brussels some 30 minutes

Oblt. Rudolf Schoenert received his Ritterkreuz on July 1, 1942.

later, a machine-gunner ignited one of his fuel tanks. Eckardt gave the order to abandon the aircraft, but on climbing out deployed his chute almost immediately. The lines got caught in one of the Bf 110's tailfins and the ace went down with the aircraft, crashing in a field at Kampenhout. Eckardt was the first Ritterkreuzträger of the Nachtjagd to fall in combat. Another 7./NJG 3 ace, Hptm. Karl Helmer, was killed during the same raid, crashing while attempting a forced landing.

The death of the Staffelkapitän seemed to coincide with the departure of 7./NJG 3 to the north of the Reich, with Laon and the border region now covered by II./NJG 4 (Hptm. Wilhelm Herget) based at Athies and III./NJG 4 (Maj. Kurt Holler) at Juvincourt. Together with II./NJG 1 at Saint-Trond, these three Gruppen were supposed to provide more or less adequate coverage of Raum 7, i.e., roughly Wallonia and the northern part of France.

Three Ritterkreuze were awarded to the Nachtjagd during the month of July: on the 1st, to Oblt. Ludwig Becker, Staka of 6./NJG 2, for his 25 victories and to Oblt. Reinhold Knacke, Staka of 1./NJG 1, for his 23 *Luftsiege*; and on 25th, to Oblt. Rudolf Schoenert, Staka 4./NJG 2, for his 21 successes.

In August, activity continued unabated with 96 *Luftsiege* claimed by the Nachtjagd which lost 15 aircraft in combat missions. Among those killed were Hptm. Herbert Bönsch, Kommandeur of III./NJG 2 (it is not known who succeeded him). A recent Ritterkreuzträger, Oblt. Reinhold Knacke, had to bail out on the night of August 15/16 and was injured. At around 03:30, he had come in underneath a Lancaster at an altitude of 5,100 meters some two kilometers east of Kevelaer in the Netherlands and set it ablaze. As he fell back behind the huge bomber—"a frightful yet majestic sight, as the flames that had started around the wing roots streamed back across and over the tail plane"—a burst of tracer was unleashed in his direction, "like flakes of snow splattering against a car's windscreen at night, luminous in the headlights." Knacke then immediately threw the stick forward and plunged down and away. Forced to shut down the starboard engine, then unable to feather the propeller, he gave the order to bail out. BF Bundrock landed safely but the pilot suffered an injury to his foot that kept him off the flight roster for several weeks.

Oblt. Reinhold Eckardt was killed on July 29/30 at Kampenhout after winning his last three victories. He had received the Ritterkreuz on August 30, 1941, and was credited with 22 victories (including three as a Zerstörer pilot). He was posthumously promoted to Hptm.

In Profile:
Hans Autenrieth

Born on March 15, 1921 in Weiler/Blaubeuren, Hans Autenrieth joined the Luftwaffe at the end of 1939. Trained as a night fighter, he soon teamed up with his radio officer, Uffz. Rudolf Adam. In June 1941, both were transferred to 6./NJG 1 and scored their first victory over Germany on August 13. At the beginning of 1942, the two comrades reached Saint-Trond with their Gruppe, being among those who escorted the *Scharnhorst* and *Gneisenau* over the Channel during Operation *Donnerkeil* in February of that year. Victory followed victory. After eight *Abschüsse*, the Autenrieth/Adam crew was transferred at the end of 1942 to 6./NJG 4 based at Tavaux. On March 8, 1943, Lt. Autenrieth scored his first "French" victory. With fewer intruders in northern France, Autenrieth and his teammate returned to Saint-Trond in the last half of 1943 to support II./NJG 1 and win further victories. They sometimes flew Do 217s. To do this, they were joined by a machine-gunner, Uffz. Georg Helbig. In January 1944, the three airmen returned to France, but soon left to temporarily defend Berlin. Two victories were scored over the capital of the Reich. However, on one occasion, the crew, now flying Bf 110 G-4s, had to evacuate their twin-engined aircraft, which had been damaged in combat. When the Gruppe returned to

Autenrieth and Adam seen here in II./NJG 1. Note the roman numeral "II" displayed on the nose of the aircraft.

Tavaux in February 1944, Autenrieth was promoted to Hptm. and Staka of 6./NJG 4. Victories and lost opportunities followed one another until June 6, 1944, when the unit was mainly converted to Ju 88 G-1s. Now operating from Coulommiers, Autenrieth flew over the D-Day beaches. Although the orders given were sometimes chaotic (on one nighttime sortie he was ordered with his Staffel to strafe the troops who had landed in the Bay of Mont Saint-Michel!) Autenrieth scored two more victories up until the night of August 3/4. While on patrol in the Avranches/Rennes sector, his Ju 88 was hit by Allied AA before the damaged twin was shot down by a Mosquito. Autenrieth and his comrades jumped but Adam was reported missing (probably murdered by civilians) while Helbig, although captured by the US Army like his pilot, also disappeared. Released from captivity in March 1946, Autenrieth worked in a variety of occupations before joining the Bundesluftwaffe 10 years later. He died in retirement on June 8, 1996. He was credited with 22 "kills."

Autenrieth relaying his instructions prior to a sortie.

Despite the losses and the difficulties of the moment, young aces began to emerge such as Lt. Hans Autenrieth who, based with II./NJG 1 at Saint-Trond, achieved six victories by the end of August (see textbox).

Faced with the increased offensive of Bomber Command, the Luftwaffe had to create new units in September 1942, despite its crying lack of resources: the Stab/NJG 5 was set up at Döberitz with Maj. Fritz Schäfer as Kommodore (little is known about him); at the same time, I./NJG 5 was formed in Stendal on the basis of II./ZG 2. Kommandeur was Hptm. Siegfried Wandam. NJG 5 was assigned the code C9+.

In September, Maj. Wilhelm Herget departed II./NJG 4 to take charge at Athies of a new I./NJG 4, the first having very probably been dissolved several months previously. This second I./NJG 4 was again composed of a very mixed group: 1./NJG 4, formerly 9/NJG 1, 2./NJG 4, was renumbered from 2./NJG 3, and 3./NJG 4 was the old 9./NJG 4. The Gruppe quickly started operations on the brand-new airfield constructed at Florennes.

At Athies, Kommandeur Herget had initially decorated his Bf 110 with a shark's mouth recalling his time in II./ZG 76. However, the decoration proved too conspicuous during night flights, forcing him to abandon it.

Raum 7—Night Fighter Base at Florennes

From the outset, the Luftwaffe had identified the large gap in the night fighter's defensive line (the Riegel) between the airfields at Saint-Trond (II./NJG 1) and Laon (Athies, II./NJG 4—Juvincourt, III./NJG 4). From these three airfields, the Bf 110s flew over Raum 7 (mainly Wallonia), but this was only a stopgap measure. The decision was taken to build a brand-new airfield right in the heart of Raum 7. At the beginning of 1942, the Florennes plateau near Namur was finally chosen. Preparations began in March 1942, but it was not until around eight months later that the runway was finally completed and the first sorties could be flown by the Bf 110s of the new I./NJG 4. According to the Gruppenadjudant of I./NJG 4, Oblt. Ludwig Meister: "My first flight from Athies to Florennes was on October 12, 1942. That day I flew as a passenger in a Fi 156 piloted by my Kommandeur Herget. We were the first to land at Florennes. Later, and on several occasions, we returned in Bf 110s. We came from Athies and dropped in to check on the progress of the work. We had to assess when we would be able to set up on this new airfield." Faced with the growing strength of Bomber Command, the German High Command nevertheless had to be patient.

Created from scratch and operational by early 1943, Florennes was to become an important night fighter base. Here, a Bf 110 is seen overflying the airfield still under construction.

An aerial view of the Florennes airbase.

After being awarded the Ritterkreuz, Ofw. Köster was granted leave to spend time with his family in Westphalia.

Paul Semrau, an ace in I./NJG 2, also received the Ritterkreuz in October 1942.

During September some 100 victories were attributed to the Nachtjagd for the loss of just five aircraft.

In October, awards were presented to the following Nachtjagd pilots: Hptm. Heinrich zu Sayn-Wittgenstein, Staka of 9./NJG 2, for his 22 victories; Hptm. Paul Semrau, Staka of 3./NJG 2 fighting in Africa—Semrau had 14 victories; Lt. Heinz Strüning, 7./NJG 2, with 24 victories; and Ofw. Alfons Köster of I./NJG 2, veteran of incursions over England and holder of 14 victories.

The Nachtjagd continued to evolve albeit somewhat haphazardly. New units were established by the "usual" expedient of splitting or renaming older formations. On October 1, II./NJG 2 became IV./NJG 1, based in Leeuwarden and headed by Maj. Helmut Lent. A new II./NJG 2 was then formed in Gilze-Rijen (Stab II./NJG 2 = Stab III./NJG 2, 4./NJG 2 = ex 7./NJG 2, and 5./NJG 2 = ex 1./NJG 2). However, it was not until August 1943 that a 6th Staffel was added.

As bad weather began to hamper operations, 39 victories were awarded to the Nachtjagd, whose losses in combat were limited to four aircraft. In November, 12 victories were awarded to the night fighters, which lost a single Bf 110 F-4 and a lone Do 217 in combat.

The Luftwaffe again took advantage of this calmer period to set up IV./NJG 3 at Grove. Although the Stab and 12./NJG 3 were created from scratch, the other two Staffeln were again drawn largely from NJG 2: 10./NJG 3 = 1./NJG 2 and 11./NJG 3 = 9/NJG 2. Kommandeur was Maj. Erich Simon, ex-Staka of 8./NJG 2, with eight victories.

In December, a II./NJG 5 was raised in Parchim. The Stab, led by the recently appointed Ritterkreuzträger Schoenert, was new, as was 6./NJG 5. The 4th Staffel came from 7./NJG 3 and 5./NJG 5 from 3./NJG 2.

Also that month a new IV./NJG 5 was established at Lechfeld, under Maj. Heinrich Prinz zu Sayn-Wittgenstein. The redesignated 2./NJG 4 became 12./NJG 5 but the two remaining Staffeln of this new Gruppe were set up with new personnel.

Despite the very bad weather that winter, December was more competitive, with 45 victories going to the Nachtjagd, which lost six aircraft in combat. It was during this month that the 22-year-old Oblt. Paul Zorner was appointed Staffelkapitän of 2./NJG 3 based on the North German coast at Wittmundhafen. He had been a frontline night fighter for some six months, flown 12 combat sorties and had, in his own words, "achieved nothing." According to his memoir, he enjoyed his role ... up to a point. His Staffel flew the Dornier Do 217. A former Ju 52 transport pilot, Zorner never liked the Do 217—the idea that it could be used as a night fighter he found preposterous as he recalled in his memoirs:

> Anyone who has progressed up the ranks would probably recall his time as Staffelkapitän most fondly. While in charge of around 100 men, this was not so many that you couldn't get to know everybody and your superiors were usually far enough away that you didn't have to have daily contact with them. In Wittmundhafen I benefited from the fact that my Staffel had hardly any older crews. This probably explained why it was entrusted to me even though I had not yet returned a single night air victory, which must have been quite unique

A II./NJG 1 Bf 110 wrecked probably following a landing accident.

in the Luftwaffe up to that point. The only downside of my new post was the aeroplane we flew—the Dornier Do 217 … Opinions on the aircraft were divided. On the one hand, it had an endurance of some six hours, was roomy, and a very stable platform for blind-flying. *Aber ein Nachtjäger? Dieser Klotz?* But a night fighter? This monstrosity? It took some 35 minutes to reach the altitude at which the bombers operated, climbing at some 6 m/sec. The Ju 88 could climb twice as fast. Although the Dornier did have air-cooled engines that could take some damage. But, along with my former Gruppe in Grove (IV./NJG 3 under Hptm.

A IV./NJG 3 Do 217 J-2 in Grove.

> Erich Simon), my 2./NJG 3 was the only unit in the entire night fighter arm that had to grapple with this 14-tonne "beer bottle." [Author's note: the empty weight of the Do 217 J was around 13,500 kg, and the max TOW was 15,400 kg.] The powers-that-be must have thought that in me they were sending an experienced man to the right place. I thought wistfully back to the Bf 110 that I had got to know and love at night fighter school … a real thoroughbred. I'd only been with my new Staffel a few days when we had the first serious accident—during the night of December 6/7, Fw. Erich Rösner crashed on takeoff and on the following night Fw. Johann Scherf's Dornier crashed on approach some 4 km from the airfield. There were no survivors among the three-man crew.

Oblt. Zorner continued to pester his Kommandeur Lippe-Weissenfeld to fly the Bf 110 and just after the turn of the year a new 110 arrived at the unit. Zorner was "authorized" to fly the Bf 110 in combat only when there was "no chance" of success with the Dornier.

In the Mediterranean theater, although 14 victories were achieved in July (including three by Hptm. Semrau), at least three crews were lost, including that of Lt. Georg Wiedow, who had shortly before been credited with two Wellingtons.

In September, the I./NJG 2, probably exhausted, reached the Belgian airfield of Melsbroek, 57 members of the unit having perished in the Mediterranean, while some 40 victories were claimed.

Based on the Do 217 E bomber, the Do 217 J was powered by the same BMW radial engines and retained the heavy rear turret. This particular machine, lacking radar or armament, coded "C3+CT" probably served with a NJ Schule 1, prior to this unit becoming NJG 101.

The crews were then engaged at night over Belgium in pure fighter operations, with three victories in September and one in October. Ofw. Robert Lüddeke was credited with two Stirlings … which were not included in his official list of victories!

On October 7, a ceremony was held at Melsbroek in honour of Hptm. Semrau, who was awarded the Ritterkreuz for his 14 victories. On the 29th, it was at Gilze-Rijen that Kammhuber presented the Ritterkreuz to Lt. Heinz Strüning (14 victories) and Ofw. Alfons Köster (11 victories).

Continuing the *Fernnachtjagd* of the previous year, crews were occasionally sent to England, mainly to drop bombs.

Following the Allied landings in North Africa, the Wehrmacht invaded the French *Zone Libre* but, short of manpower, the Luftwaffe called up I./NJG 2 (temporarily led by Hptm. Horst Patuschka) at Cazaux on November 9. The Ju 88 Cs patrolled (for fear of invasion) along the coast without much trouble, but the unit was now to be split up. At the end of November, the 1/NJG 2 moved to Foggia to be assigned to the newly formed II/NJG 2 (which was in turn assigned to the Mediterranean), thus becoming its 5th Staffel. On December 10, 2 and 3./NJG 2 returned to Melsbroek. A second 1./NJG 2 was reformed within the unit … before becoming 10./NJG 3 and being reborn a few weeks later thanks to the efforts of the Gruppe.

Parade at Melsbroek in October 1942 at I./NJG 2 as Hptm. Semrau is presented with the Ritterkreuz by General Kammhuber.

Nachtjagd Units, December 1942

Stab/NJG 1: Deelen

I./NJG 1: Venlo

II./NJG 1: Saint-Trond

III./NJG 1: Twente

IV./NJG 1: Leeuwarden

Stab/NJG 2: Comiso

I./NJG 2: Cazaux

II./NJG 2: Comiso

Stab/NJG 3: Stade

I./NJG 3: Vechta

II./NJG 3: Schleswig

III./NJG 3: Stade

IV./NJG 3: Grove

Stab/NJG 4: Metz

I./NJG 4: Athies (Florennes)

II./NJG 4: Saint-Dizier

III./NJG 4: Juvincourt

Stab/NJG 5: Döberitz

I./NJG 5: Stendal

II./NJG 5: Parchim

Various smaller formations deployed over the Eastern Front mostly engaged in "anti-partisan" operations

The German night fighter arm had not done badly in 1942—according to one account some 65 percent of contacts had resulted in downings. The Nachtjagd had a (theoretical) strength of some five Geschwader (amounting to 15 Gruppen) and was supported by a virtually seamless and highly effective ground infrastructure, albeit a very costly one. In early 1943 there was relatively little activity in the night skies over Germany. It was the calm before the storm announced in threatening terms by Arthur Harris in leaflet drops over German cities.

In Profile:
Do 217 Night Fighters

Dornier Do 217 J-2 coded "D5+AM" was based on the north German coast during the fall of 1942. The J variant was powered by BMW radials and retained the Do 217 bomber's rear DL 131 electric upper turret and featured a defensive lower gondola. It was slow and heavy and not liked much by the NJG 3 crews that flew it. The Dornier Do 217 N-2 (below) was a different beast—made lighter and powered by the inline liquid-cooled DB 603A, one of the most powerful 12-cylinder engines in Luftwaffe service, which conferred superior performance. Here it is fitted with the FuG 202 Matratze radar array and a quartet of slanting weapons. Note the N-2 has no rear turret, and the ventral gondola is also faired over. At the time it was probably the biggest and most heavily armed "fighter" ever put into service.

Battle for the Ruhr: January–June 1943

With the wider war turning against Germany—Stalingrad, El Alamein—Roosevelt and Churchill had set out their plans at Casablanca for a round-the-clock bombing campaign against Germany. With the Americans operating by day, Harris and Bomber Command were about to launch an all-out offensive aimed at the "progressive destruction and dislocation of the German military, industrial, and economic system." First to be targeted with renewed impetus was the Ruhr industrial district which provided Germany with most of its coal and electricity—aided by Oboe bomb-aiming and navigation technology and Bennett's Pathfinders, now a bomber group in their own right. The average German night fighter knew none of this, far less that he would soon be committed during daylight raids—with terrible consequences.

On the night of January 24/25, 1943, Lt. Wolfgang Kuthe (11./NJG 1) shot down this Lancaster of 460 Sqn at Warns, Netherlands, his third victory. He went on to return eight *Luftsiege* before being killed on April 14, 1943.

At the beginning of the year, the Nachtjagd was augmented by the addition of a new Gruppe, IV./NJG 4, which was established in Mainz-Finthen under the command of Maj. Heinrich Wohlers. Only 12. Staffel was created from scratch, 10. and 11. Staffeln formed from 8. and 6./NJG 4. Wohlers had seven confirmed victories at the time and more than likely owed his position to his organizational skills. For its part, IV./NJG 5 left Lechfeld for Insterburg, passing from the command of Jafü Süddeutschland to that of Ostpreussen. With bad weather hampering operations, the Nachtjagd reportedly lost only five aircraft in combat in January (often with their crews killed). One Do 217 was mistakenly shot down by German Flak.

As for the *Luftsiege*, no fewer than 48 bombers were reported to have been shot down by the Nachtjagd. While a few young aces appeared (such as Lt. Wolfgang Kuthe of 11./NJG 1, who won his fifth victory at the end of the month), the *Experten* continued to add to their record of achievements (Oblt. Ludwig Becker: 44 "kills;" Hptm. Reinhold Knacke: 42; Hptm. Prinz zur Lippe: 39).

On January 17, 1943, some 190 RAF bombers raided Berlin. Oblt. Paul Zorner was airborne for his 14th combat sortie as a Nachtjäger:

> just after 20:00 my BF Wilke and myself were sent to patrol in Raum Jaguar out over the coast under JLO Oblt. Jansen. We orbited the beacon, now flying clockwise, then going around counterclockwise. Nothing was happening. Impatiently I radioed every two minutes or so to ask Jansen about the *Luftlage*—the situation in the air. Every time Jansen reported back from his Seeburgtisch that the British were flying out over Helgoland far to the north. And then after 90 minutes of waiting, an instruction: "*Antreten, Kurs 45 Grad … Entfernung 30.*" We had barely received the order than I opened the throttles, turning onto a heading of 45 degrees. An enemy machine some 30 km ahead of us. Jansen reported one of the bombers flying home was much farther south than the rest. We were given various corrections from the ground station … Jansen brought us elegantly in behind the bomber which was flying at an altitude of 3,200 meters. We had closed to 3 km. By now on a westerly heading, I kept lower at 3,000 m. Tension in the cockpit was now at its highest. The temperature gauge was showing -26° outside but in my flying suit I was sweating. I prepared my armament for action, took off the safety and adjusted the brightness of the gunsight while Wilke worked on his search radar. Outside the sky was cloudless, the moon hung low in the southeast and below us everything was gray—we were some 35 km out over the sea. "*Entfernung 1.8, geradeaus*—1,800 meters, straight ahead." Wilke still had nothing on his scope. And then, "*Wilke, da ist er!*" Wilke reported to the ground station, "*Wir berühren* … we have contact." Gradually the gray shadow drew closer. At 400 m the exhaust flames from four engines were visible from directly astern, even with flame suppressors. At 150 m the bomber was still flying straight and level. His wings grew larger and larger out of the circle of the sight. It seemed impossible that they hadn't caught sight of us. And then it was time. At some 70 meters astern and slightly below the bomber I throttled back subconsciously, tightened my grip on the stick a little and curled the index finger of my right hand around the firing button. The cannons barked briefly. With no apparent effect, the bomber continued straight and level. By now the distance separating us was down to 40 meters. A second burst, pulling the nose up and letting the port wing fly through the crosshairs. I saw flashes of explosions, but immediately had to throttle back and pull away to the left to avoid ramming the bomber. It rolled over on its left side and after a few seconds went down in a steep spiral.

Oblt. Paul Zorner seen at the controls of his Bf 110.

The Americans had already flown their first daylight raids over mainland Europe during 1942 and it was only a matter of time before huge armadas of bombers were launched against targets in Germany itself. On January 27, 1943, US Eighth Air Force B-17 Fortresses escorted by P-38s hit U-boat yards in Vegesack. With Luftwaffe fighter Gruppen deployed on many far-flung fronts and only a handful of units available to protect the homeland, the night fighters with their good endurance and heavy armament would also be thrown into the battles by day—a reckless decision as Paul Zorner explained:

> operations around the clock posed a huge psychological and physical strain … at the time I was flying a Bf 110 F-4 which may well have been the most heavily armed variant of the Messerschmitt but it could only manage 460 kph in level flight, barely 40 kph faster than a bomber formation operating at 6,500 m … We were lone fighters and achieved our night air victories against individual aircraft. Sending us up against heavily armed *Pulks* [groups or boxes], some of them operating under fighter cover … can only be described as criminal. The consequences for the Nachtjagd and its crews were not long in coming.

In February, the Nachtjagd lost 10 aircraft from NJG 1 and NJG 3. Two of the pilots killed were successful night fighter aces: on February 3, over the Netherlands, Hptm. Reinhold Knacke, Staka of 1./NJG 1, shot down his 43rd and 44th *Luftsiege*, but was killed by defensive fire from his last victim; on February 24, the left engine of IV./NJG 1 Bf 110 G-4 (coded "G9+HH" WNr. 4846) blew up as 43-victory ace Oblt. Paul Gildner gave chase to a fast, high-flying *Kurier*. Bordfunker Hans Huhn recorded in his diary:

> *Kurier* lost in Lichtenstein, contact broken, too fast. We get orders from ground to return immediately because of worsening weather. Port engine running unevenly … sudden vibration in port engine, heavy flames and sparks. Gildner stops it. Flight home on one engine … on one engine through the clouds. I transmit that our port engine is dead and request *Radischen*—emergency flares. Port engine started again, circuit to port. "I prefer to make a right-hand circuit," Gildner says. In starboard turn. A bang and a blow in the port engine, like something disintegrating. Gildner, perfectly calm, "Jump, Huhn, jump!" I'm out. I let myself go, my helmet is torn off and I'm carried away under the tailplane.

Huhn survived but Gildner was killed in the ensuing crash just north of Gilze-Rijen. He received a posthumous Eichenlaub. This aircraft was the first G-4 to be reported lost in a Nachtjagd unit.

Some 52 victories were chalked up during the month. These were achieved not only at night against the RAF—now engaging more and more aircraft in a single raid, as on the night of February 3/4 when 263 bombers went to Hamburg—but also against the USAAF. Three B-17s were shot down over the North Sea on February 4 and two B-24s on February 26.

It was on this date that the Staffelkapitän of 12./NJG 1 perished—Hptm. Ludwig Becker. Responsible for testing the new Lichtenstein BC search radar in August and September 1941 and the first pilot to achieve a Lichtenstein *Abschuss*, Becker was one of the "fathers of night-fighting" with 44 victories. He was downed by American escort fighters over Schiermonnikoog, off the coast of Holland. That same morning his award of the Eichenlaub had been confirmed along with one for Werner Streib. These three *Experten* lost in February alone—incidentally, all with the same victory totals—would be missed by the Nachtjagd in the tough battles ahead.

On February 19, 1943, Oblt. Paul Zorner achieved his third victory—this time at the controls of a Do 217. Climbing out over the North Sea that night, he was vectored towards a mine-laying Wellington some 12 km north of Norderney. Approaching the Wellington head on, the two aircraft banked into a "turning fight" that lasted some 20 minutes as Zorner vainly sought to draw a bead on the British twin, hauling back with all his might on the stick in the turn, even getting the flight mechanic to help him maintain his effort on the control column. To achieve an outcome, Zorner had to resort to desperate measures—giving the order to dump some 800 kg of fuel to lighten the Dornier, a risk worth taking as they were only some 35 km from base. Putting in a superhuman effort on the stick he managed a brief burst of fire which sent the Wellington down. There were no witnesses in the air—the downing was later confirmed by a Flak battery. Zorner and crew then had to nurse their "fighter" home on just one engine some 100 m above the waves—a single round the size of a $1 coin had punctured an oil line. As Zorner put it later: "When we landed, I went and saw the Kommandeur Lippe-Weissenfeld and told him exactly what I thought of the Do 217." Zorner never flew the aircraft again at night.

Aware of the growing power of the RAF and USAAF and the lack of manpower in the night defense, German officials tried to strengthen the Nachtjagd by creating a new Geschwader. NJG 101 was in fact just the rebranding of a training school: the Nachtjagdschule 1.

The Stab/NJG 101 remained in Schleissheim under the command of Ob. Rudolf Stoltenhoff. I./NJG 101, also in Schleissheim, was led by a veteran Zerstörer pilot, Hptm. Theodor Rossiwall. II./NJG 101 based at Munich-Riem was commanded by Maj. Hans-Dietrich Knoetzsch. A former Fieseler test pilot, he had led I./NJG 3 in 1941/42. III./NJG 101 of Hptm. Helmut Peters was at Stuttgart-Echterdingen. Peters was also a former Zerstörer pilot who had led 1./NJG 3 in 1940. In short, very good officers/pilots but few with real combat experience.

Despite efforts at the highest levels, this reinforcement was rather weak in the face of the new threat. On the night of March 5/6 1943, Bomber Command launched the so-called "battle of the Ruhr," an intensive attack on the industrial heartland of the Reich. A raid on one of the most heavily defended of German cities, Essen, was flown during that night by over 400 aircraft and directed at the Krupps steelworks in the center of the city.

Reinhold Knacke was killed on the night of February 3/4, 1943, hit by the return fire from an RAF bomber.

Gebetsandenken
an den gefallenen Flieger

Otto Hagn

Schmiedmeisterssohn
von Oberbergkirchen

Feldwebel und Flugzeugführer in einer Nacht-Jagdstaffel

Inh. der Erinnerungsmed. von Oesterreich und Sudetenland sowie der Frontflugspange

der am 20. Febr. 1943 bei einem Luftkampf im Alter von 23 Jahren in der Nordsee den Heldentod starb.

Du warst so gut, starbst viel zu früh,
Solch braves Herz vergißt man nie;
Wer ihn kannte, liebte ihn,
Wer Liebe hat, der bet' für ihn.
Drum ruhe sanft in fremder Erde,
Geliebter Sohn und Bruder, du,
Bis wir dich einstens sehen werden
In des Himmels ewiger Ruh'.

D. Geiger, Mühldorf.

On the night of February 18/19, Wilhelmshaven suffered one of the many attacks of the period. Two Lancasters from a force of 195 bombers were shot down by the Nachtjagd, which lost two aircraft, including Fw. Hagn's Bf 110, which came down in the sea off Sankt Peter.

Oblt. Rudolf Sigmund (10./NJG 1) was one of the two pilots who may have downed a B-24 by day over the North Sea on February 26, 1942. Having achieved some 28 "kills" and been awarded the Ritterkreuz, he was shot down and killed as Kommandeur of III./NJG 3 on the night of October 4/5, 1943.

Bf 110 D/F coded "R4+CC" (possibly WNr. 3482) flown by Oblt. Rudolf Sigmund, September/October 1942. Note the eight white *Abschussbalken* victory markings on the tailfin. (Rob de Visser collection via Theo Boiten)

Having led NJS 1, Obst. Rudolf Stoltenhoff was appointed Kommodore of the new NJG 101. A prewar pilot, he had commanded I./JG 54 in 1939 before moving to the Zerstörer arm. A good organizer of a second-line unit, he would now have to lead his men in a disproportionate battle.

The night fighters caught six bombers returning through the *Himmelbett* chain—up from Leeuwarden, the Kommandeur of IV./NJG 1, Maj. Helmut Lent, returned his 60th and 61st victories. It would be the first of some 31 major raids flown against towns in the Ruhr up to the end of July, while a further 20 raids were flown against other targets.

During that month, the Nachtjagd lost 13 Bf 110/Do 217 twins, claiming 96 *Abschüsse*, a high figure indicating something of the scale of the increasing intrusions by Allied air forces. Three B-17s were claimed over the North Sea on March 4 by III./NJG 1 and a B-24 over the Jade Bight on Germany's North Sea coast on March 18. Oblt. Paul Zorner, Staka of 3./NJG 3, flew his first day sortie on March 22, 1943, managing five frontal passes against the four-engined bombers for no visible effect.

At the end of the month, I./NJG 4 was able to start occupying the new Fliegerhorst at Florennes. According to Gruppe adjutant, Oblt. Ludwig Meister:

> On March 29, I./NJG 4 left Athies to set up in Florennes. There was only one runway in good condition, running from east to west, and on both sides, work was in full swing with many vehicles of all kinds. You had to land precisely in line with the runway. Otherwise, if you touched down on the left or the right, the planes were likely to turn over, their landing gear blocked by the mud. Fortunately, there were very few accidents. Our crews were well trained, and everything went off without a hitch.

Initially, only the Stab and 1./NJG 4 moved. The 2./NJG 4 followed shortly afterwards but, at that time, 3./NJG 4 (still equipped with heavy Do 217s that could not yet land at Florennes) remained in France.

Do 217 N-2 coded "3C+HR" of 7./NJG 4. Although criticized by some crews, this heavy aircraft was used throughout 1943. The *Schräge Musik* cannon installation is visible behind the streamlined fairing bult into the design with the removal of the upper gun turret. (via Taghon)

The Dornier Do 217 N-2 was the final Dornier night fighter variant. In addition to *Schräge Musik* there was a quartet of MG 151/20 cannon in the nose. (Stipdonk)

On the night of March 29/30, 1943, Lt. August Geiger (7./NJG 1) returned his *Luftsiege* 15–19 over the course of two sorties. He was to receive the Ritterkreuz on May 22 for 26 victories but was killed on the night of September 28/29, 1943 by an intruder night fighter. At that time his "score" was 54 *Abschüsse*.

Adler in die Lüfte steigen
Flieger von den Taten schweigen
Einsam ist der Wolken Weg!

Unser unvergeßlicher
Sohn und Bruder
Unteroffizier
Christl Költringer
Flugzeugführer in einem
Nachtjagdgeschwader
Träger des EK 2 und der
Frontflugspange
welcher im Alter von 22 Jahren
bei einem schweren Luftkampf
in Holland den Fliegertod fand.

Du gabst dein junges und erfolgreiches Leben für deine Heimat.

Herr, ganz dein Wille geschehe.

Süßes Herz Maria, sei seine Rettung!

During the night of March 29/30, Uffz. Christian Költringer (7./NJG 1) was shot down and killed with his radio operator in combat with an RAF bomber over Vriezenveen. He had been awarded the EK II for his three victories over the Netherlands earlier in the year.

On the evening of March 11, 1943, some 314 Halifax, Lancaster, and Stirling bombers were dispatched to attack Stuttgart. Bordfunker Karl Johanssen flew his third combat sortie, a ground control intercept in Raum Bergziege. His own pilot was sick, so he was flying with Lt. Johannes Engels, a 10. Staffel old hand ("*ein alter Hase*"):

> We were still a young novice crew fresh out of training when we arrived in Mainz-Finthen at III./NJG 4 in January 1943. We eagerly flew more training flights and were proud when the "*alter Hasen*"—operating out of Eindhoven or now and again from our own field—returned victories flying the *Himmelbett* procedure. After countless practice target sorties in the different "boxes" (*Räume*) such as "Dachs," "Kauz," "Nachtigall," and "Bergziege" we were finally due for assignment to a mission. It was of course the experienced crews who always took off ahead of the rest in the first wave when incursions were reported. To then be dispatched to a "box" as a "reward" as I was during the return flight of the enemy aircraft was quite an event. We had collected a new Bf 110 F coded "2Z+IU" in Gilze-Rijn and it was fitted out with a new piece of electronic equipment—the Lichtenstein search radar. We did one 40-minute practice flight in the vicinity of the airfield and then on March 11, 1943 we went to cockpit readiness (*Sitzbereitschaft*). At 21:43 we were ordered up and got airborne and headed for the Bergziege box.

Johanssen's radio link with the JLO was working well and the Bf 110 climbed quickly to its assigned altitude of 5,300 meters. All the equipment was checked and the onboard armament of four MGs and two MG FF 2-cm cannon was readied for operation. At his radio operator's feet were the clip-in ammunition drums for the two 2-cm cannon, each with 75 rounds.

On the Lichtenstein's sighting screen, the reference lines and the ground "spikes" glowed in green, indicating the Bf 110's own altitude at the same time. Arriving at the Bergziege radio beacon, the crew were sent to the northwestern "border" of the box and orbited there in wide circles to wait for further instructions.

> Finally, we received instructions from the JLO to begin our approach. Our changes of heading and altitude were relayed as we had practiced during our training sorties using the usual key words—*zwei mal* Lisa ("20° to the left"), Marie 7 ("7 km dead astern on the same heading"), Hanni 5.2 ("altitude 5,200 meters"), *eins mal* Rolf ("right 10°"), Lisa ("left 10°"). The Lichtenstein was still not of any help at this stage. Hopefully we could intercept the "*dicke Auto*" (fat car) before it had the left the area covered by the ground Würzburg radar. "Rolf—Marie 4—Lisa"—"a few more degrees to the left." Suddenly our IU was rocked by turbulence—the prop wash of a bomber. And there on the "Li" screen a new return had popped up—it must be the enemy bomber. The ground controller continued to broadcast his instructions, but the pilot was now only listening to mine. "*Rolf, mehr Rolf, Stop. Etwas Lisa* [a little to the left], *gleiche Höhe, etwas Siegfried* [climb a little]." With a hard control movement, the *Kutscher* called out: "*Da ist er!*—there he is!" Then, calling the ground station; "*Wir machen Pauke Pauke*!—we are attacking!" Our eyes were now outside and searching for the "black box." Small bluish exhaust flames made it easier for us to keep it in sight. Four engines, twin tails—these thoughts lodged in our minds. From around 200 meters behind and below to the right of the bomber, we unleashed our first salvoes—with no apparent effect. But they knew we were there, and the four-engined bomber was firing back and making evasive maneuvers. Our second burst of fire. The tracers disappeared into the wing and fuselage. We must have hurt it! More twisting and turning, another burst of fire, but these maneuvers had left us in the gunners' sights. There was a crackling sound in our IU. Our starboard engine was now trailing a plume of white smoke. *Kühlstoff*—coolant leak!

With his engine hit but still running, Engels flew another attack from below and the left side. A burst of fire from his four MGs slammed home. But then as the Bf 110 turned to the right under the enemy machine, the RAF bomber dropped its nose at that same moment. The port wingtip of the Bf 110 clipped the bomber's right wing. Johanssen: "There was a sharp quick blow—*wir fliegen noch*. We were still flying. The starboard engine chose this moment to stop. The bomber had turned away to the left and while I tried to raise the ground controller on the frequency and give the 'driver' a heading to the nearest radio beacon, the cockpit was suddenly lit up by a bright light—*die Feindmaschine ist abgestürzt*. The bomber had plunged to the ground and the impact fire now glowed brightly in the wooded and mountainous terrain. We were still at 800 meters—below us, a few jagged mountain peaks in the haze and above them a clear starry sky with a crescent moon. All these perceptions were interrupted by a sudden shout over the intercom (EiV): 'Johanssen, *Aussteigen!* Johanssen, bail out, I can't hold the aircraft any longer.'"

Both Uffz. Johanssen and his pilot successfully evacuated their stricken Bf 110 F-4. Their victim, a 405 Sqn Halifax, came down near Heidelberg. Later that day, on the evening of March 12, Johanssen flew out in a Fieseler Storch to inspect the wreckage of the bomber. It was his first *Abschussbeteiligung*—or "victory participation." The following month he would be teamed up with Oblt. Martin Becker (pilot) and went on to share in a further 57 victories.

In Profile:
Ju 88 C NJG 1

Junkers Ju 88 C-6 "R4+FM" of 10./NJG 1 flown by Oblt. and Ritterkreuzträger Wilhelm Beier. His final claim was on the night of May 29/30, 1943, a 35 Sqn Halifax (HR 973) downed northwest of Maastricht (37th or 38th victory) and flown with BF Kurt Bundrock. According to T. Boiten, "the majority of Wilhelm Beier's 38 nighttime victory claims in WWII remain unidentified. Only around a dozen of his *Abschüsse* can be matched against RAF losses, and even of these, only seven with certainty." In other words, after Beier had received the Ritterkreuz in October 1941 (for his 14 *Fernnachtjagd Abschüsse* in 3./NJG 2) he filed a series of doubtful victory claims. Following his last two claims his Kommandeur had him "quietly transferred" to 11./NJG101, the so-called Training Command East on July 15, 1943. After a posting as a flying instructor (until August 10, 1944) he rejoined a frontline unit—7./NJG 100. He came back to the night fighter defense of Germany with 11./NJG 3, on October 7, 1944, posted to 8. Staffel at the end of the month. It is not known if he flew any further operational sorties prior to joining Ausbildungskommando 262 at Neuburg/Donau in April 1945. The camouflage finish of his C-6 appears to be RLM 71 Dunkelgrün overall broken up by irregular stripes of RLM 75 (Mittelgrau) and 74 (Dunkelgrau).

The battle of the Ruhr was in full swing, saturating the German defenses. During April, the Nachtjagd lost 15 aircraft (one hit a Lancaster on the night of 9th/10th). The number of victories—around 150—was an indication of the intensity of the fighting. On the night of April 10/11, Kommandeur Herget (I./NJG 4) returned the first victory flying out of Florennes, downing a 426 Sqn Wellington over Virelles. According to R. Charlier:

> the target that night was Frankfurt am Main. The attack was not a success, the bombs scattering across the countryside. Shortly after 03:00, Herget's radio operator, Fw. Hans Liebherr, was alerted to enemy aircraft in Raum 7. He warned his pilot, who headed in the direction indicated. The two Würzburg radars near Chimay followed the aircraft. Liebherr's contact was a Wellington returning home and as the Bf 110 closed, the Hptm. opened fire. The pilot of the Canadian aircraft flew desperate maneuvers to escape the deadly fire. The twin-engined plane burst into flames while the pilot anxiously sought out an area to put down on. The Wellington orbited Virelles, passing over the town twice before exploding at 03:23 and crashing on the edge of the Virelles woods. Four bodies were found in the wood where the fuselage had come down. A fifth, that of the rear gunner, lay in a meadow where the detached tail of the bomber had crashed.

Herget was soon guided onto another return on Liebherr's scopes and downed a second Wellington near Laon for his 28th victory. Another Kommandeur, Maj. Walter Ehle (II./NJG 1), shot down a Stirling of 7 Sqn at Tongerlo.

A memorial card issued postwar in honor of the crew of the Wellington of 426 Sqn shot down at Virelles on the night of April 10/11 by the Kommandeur of I./NJG 4, Hptm. Wilhelm Herget (his 27th victory).

The Bf 110 of Hptm. Walter Borchers, Kommandeur of the brand-new III./NJG 5.

On the night of April 16/17, 37 bombers were claimed by the Nachtjagd during a long-range raid on the Czech Skoda armaments factory in Pilsen. On April 17, Oblt. Zorner was again committed by day against American bomber formations raiding Bremen, attacking a *Pulk* with two head-on firing passes. He was hit by return fire in the wing and both engines started to stream coolant. Forced to shut both down and feather his props, he glided from an altitude of 7,000 meters to carry out a successful belly landing. Three B-17s were confirmed downed by NJG 1 and NJG 3. However, it was soon decided that those night fighter aces with 10 or more victories should not be committed by day.

A III. Gruppe of NJG 5 was set up in Neuruppin in April, headed by Hptm. Walter Borchers. The 3. Staffeln were only raised with new personnel from the schools. On April 16, the Ritterkreuz was awarded to Oblt. Manfred Meurer, the Staka of 3./NJG 1, who by now had chalked up 23 "kills."

A Defection From NJG 3

During early 1943, Junkers was finally able to bring the Junkers Ju 88 into production with the air-cooled BMW 801. Compared to the Jumo 211, the A to D series of the BMW 801 had a higher takeoff power of 1600 hp. The Ju 88 R series fighters were basically versions of the Ju 88 C-6, powered by BMW 801 radial engines. Based on the Nachtjäger Ju 88 C-4 and C-6, the Junkers modifications of the BMW 801 engine led to the initial designations C-4/R1 and C-6/R2. These aircraft were soon given their own series designations R-1 and R-2. The R-1 had 1,539-hp BMW 801 L engines and the R-2 was powered by 1,677-hp BMW 801 G-2 engines.

One of the first aircraft from the R-1 series that went into service (WNr. 360 043) was involved in one of the most significant defections from the Luftwaffe. On May 9, 1943, Ju 88 R-1 coded "D5+EV," which was stationed with 10./NJG 3 in Aalborg, Denmark, flew to RAF Dyce in Scotland (now Aberdeen Airport) with its entire crew and suite of electronic equipment on board, including the highly secret FuG 202 Lichtenstein BC search radar and associated signals books. Most postwar accounts of this defection are either contradictory or fanciful or both. One account, not previously published in English, was written by Herbert Thomas, an Uffz. in 2. Staffel of I./NJG 2 during early 1941:

> During 1940 Schmid, Rosenberger and Kantwill were my roommates in our barracks accommodation in Gilze-Rijen. Schmid and Rosenberger were loners and kept themselves to themselves (*Sie galten in unserem Kreis as Einzelgänger*). When we weren't flying, they were never there, and were certainly never part of our "crowd." Nobody thought anything of it at the time. Only Kantwill regularly complained that his two "fugitives" had disappeared yet again. This, of course, was played up even more by us, to the amusement of everyone present. Schmid was an experienced pilot, Rosenberger a radio operator of the old school and together they were a so-called *Friedensbesatzung*—a very competent peacetime crew. [According to some sources Oblt. Herbert Schmid flew 168 combat sorties in Spain in the Condor Legion. His awards included the Frontflugspange in Gold, the Spanienkreuz in Gold and the Wound Badge in Black]. As *Fernnachtjäger* our victory totals grew with every sortie and all the experienced crews shared in this success. Only Schmid and his crew had no luck on their combat flights.
>
> In his book *Ferne Nachtjagd* Oberstabsarzt Otto Mölenbeck reports one incident that took place on November 9, 1940—during a dusk sortie over England, Schmid's machine was seen circling over the English coast, at around 21:00. Was he attempting to defect on that day? His Dornier was driven off by RAF fighters. Had they not been informed of his "arrival"?

By late 1942 RAF bomber losses were constantly on the rise, with some 70 percent of these attributable to Würzburg and Lichtenstein—something had to be done on the British side to uncover the secrets of these systems. As is now well known a Würzburg was seized on the French coast by British commandos at Bruneval. I am certain that the British Secret Service then "negotiated" with Schmid the delivery of a Lichtenstein-equipped Ju 88 directly to the UK—this was "D5+EV"—which he then flew to Dyce ("*es gilt als sicher, dass SIS mit Schmid die Auslieferung einer entsprechende Maschine 'aushandelte', die er dann nach Dyce flog und dort ablieferte*"). Schmid took off from Denmark, refueled at Kristiansand, Norway, and was airborne again ostensibly for a sortie over the Skagerrak. The last radio contact from him was from Planquadrat (grid square) 88/41, the northwest tip of Jutland. While still in range of German radar he reported an engine fire and that he was having to ditch. That was his last communication. Schmid's Ju 88 crossed the North Sea and was "intercepted" and led into Dyce by RAF Spitfires. Just four days later the Ju 88 R was flown down to Farnborough again under escort. The secrets delivered by Schmid led directly to the British decision to deploy Window, something that up to that point they had been reluctant to do for fear of German retaliation. Window comprised short thin metal strips of chaff cut to a wavelength that would paralyze German radar. Schmid and Rosenberger later took part in Operation *Corona*—an attempt to use German language speakers to broadcast false instructions to Luftwaffe night fighters and transmit signals from "fake" radio beacons. Homing onto these could have catastrophic consequences for night fighter crews—the loss of Hans Mäckle's Ju 88 G-1 (III./NJG 2) on July 13, 1944 which landed at Woodbridge in Suffolk was one of these. Even if Schmid was opposed to the regime, there can be no excuse for his actions. He did not damage our German leadership—his defection harmed only his comrades.

Not only did the capture of WNr. 360043 lead to the jamming of the early FuG 202 and 212 sets but their tracking as well—the development of Serrate fitted to Mosquito intruders enabled the hunting down of German night fighters by tracking emissions from their Lichtenstein B/C, C-1, or later SN-2 sets. In addition, the corkscrew maneuver was developed—this widely employed defensive technique effectively removed a bomber from the 60° cone of coverage of an attacking night fighter's Lichtenstein radar.

Wilde Sau: Summer 1943

While the fighting in the Ruhr was raging in the west, the Allies were triumphing in Africa. Their bombers could now threaten the Romanian oilfields, at Ploiesti, the lifeblood of the Reich. This prospect led directly to the establishment of a new IV./NJG 6. Set up from scratch with Bf 110s and new personnel and based at Bucharest-Otopeni and Zilistea, the Gruppe was placed under the command of the recently promoted Maj. Herbert Lütje.

In the battle for the Ruhr, the Nachtjagd lost 13 aircraft. Among the airmen killed were Oblt. Lothar Linke, Staka of 12./NJG 1. After winning his last two victories, 26th/27th, on the night of May 13/14, he had to abandon his aircraft with his engines on fire. As he jumped out, he hit the tailfin of his Bf 110 and was killed. He was posthumously awarded the Ritterkreuz.

As Staka of 8./NJG 1, Hptm. Herbert Lütje had been credited with a B-17 (his 17th Abschuss) near Den Helder on a morning sortie, March 4, 1943, despite having flown that night. He was appointed Kommandeur of the newly established IV./NJG 6 in Romania, June 1943. He ended the war as Kommodore of NJG 6 credited with 50 "kills."

The new IV./NJG 6 operated out of Otopeni, Bucharest's main airfield. In correspondence with the former Staka 11./NJG 6, Oblt. Martin Bauer, the former pilot claimed that the unit's Bf 110s were painted off-white, providing better camouflage under moonlight.

Victories reached a record 158, during major RAF raids: 28 on May 4/5 during an attack on Dortmund (including the 65th and 66th for Maj. Lent leading IV./NJG 1); 24 on May 12/13 (Duisburg); 27 on May 13/14 (Bochum, Pilzen). This total included six victories for Hptm. Lütje, who was then promoted to Major to lead IV./NJG 6. His victims that night comprised three Lancaster (the first, an 83 Sqn machine, timed at 23:22) and three Halifax bombers, the last one timed at 02:55. Lütje was the first Nachtjagd pilot to down six four-engined bombers in one night. (his *Abschüsse* 23–28). He was awarded the Ritterkreuz on June 1, 1943.

Bomber Command's target for the final raid of May 1943 was Barmen-Wuppertal on the night of May 29/30. A force of some 719 bombers lost 21 aircraft to the Nachtjagd, with a further 12 probably falling victim to Flak. That was barely 4.5 percent of the force involved—an indicator of the Nachtjagd's growing shortage not only of defensive aircraft but also of experienced crews.

On May 22, Lt. August Geiger (7./NJG 1) was awarded the Ritterkreuz.

In the face of the huge numbers of RAF bombers now being committed, some Nachtjagd aces found themselves rushed from airfield to airfield to fill the gaps as recalled by Oblt. Paul Zorner:

On May 30, 1943, Oblt. Rudolf Altendorf (Staka of 2./NJG 4) drove out to the crash site of the 419 Sqn Halifax which he had shot down during the night at Péronnes-lez-Binche, Belgium. With him were male and female personnel from the radar station who had played an active part in this victory.

A Nachtjäger like many others. On the night of May 29/30, the Bf 110 G-4 of Oblt. Fritz Engau (5./NJG 1) was hit by a bomber over Belgium. Both German airmen bailed out, but Engau hit the ground hard and apparently never recovered his night vision. He subsequently switched to the Tagjagd.

Lt. Johannes Hager—seen standing (right) on the wing of a Bf 110—was shot down during the night of May 29/30 at the controls of a Do 217 but returned to his unit and ended the war with a "score" of 48 and the Ritterkreuz.

> This "idea" did not appear to be particularly well thought out. On May 12, we were deployed from Vechta to Saint-Trond, on the 13th we were sent to Leeuwarden, on the 14th to Gilze-Rijen, in the early morning of the 15th back to Saint-Trond and that same afternoon we flew back to Leeuwarden. We had seven days here before being sent back to Saint-Trond for the next five weeks. From Saint-Trond we manned a "box." An attempt was made to deploy two night fighters in certain "boxes" in order to better counter the RAF's bomber "stream" but this didn't work very well. The limitations of "guided" night-fighting were quite apparent.

Meanwhile decorated bomber pilot Hptm. Hajo Herrmann—promoting the deployment of single-engined day fighters at night to "maximize" the numbers of available night fighters—had himself taken to flying an Fw 190 at night from a Berlin airfield against RAF Mosquito intruders. He described one sortie flown during April 1943 in his memoir:

> [the Mosquito] was caught in a searchlight that would not let him go. I leveled out behind him at around 9,000 meters and pushed the throttle wide open. I saw that I was barely gaining on him … On the ground the Flak was firing off salvo after salvo. Dozens of batteries were lighting up the suburbs of Berlin. The enemy pilot knew what was coming and banked over into a tight turn before he could be caught in the first height-adjusted bursts. At full power I cut across his turn and was suddenly able to close on him very rapidly. Growing ever large in front

Former KG 30 Ju 88 bomber pilot, Hans-Joachim "Hajo" Herrmann conceived the *Wilde Sau* "freelance" night-fighting concept and flew Fw 190s in his own "Night Fighter Test Detachment Herrmann" which became JG 300, later one of the leading homeland air defense fighter wings of the Luftwaffe.

> of me and still caught in the cone of light he came within range of my MGs and cannon. I pressed the firing button … and was blinded! Stupid, bad planning! No flame suppressors, no night tracer … A few seconds later the chase was over as the Mosquito was swallowed up by the darkness. I could imagine the crew congratulating themselves on having escaped the attentions of a night fighter.

Herrmann was given the green light to set up an ad-hoc unit to test out his theories, the so-called Nachtjagdversuchskommando Herrmann (NJVK, Night Fighter Test Detachment Herrmann). Herrmann's test unit was based at Bonn-Hangelar where he set about recruiting instructors, ex-bomber and Lufthansa pilots who were experienced in blind-flying techniques. Operating with the aid of searchlights or the light from flares and thus independently of radar, this method of attack was dubbed *Wilde Sau* or "wild boar" night-fighting. It was a return of sorts to *Helle Nachtjagd* albeit this time directly over the cities under attack. And—although the Germans did not appreciate it yet—it was a tactic that could not be jammed. An officer who knew Herrmann in Berlin was Maj. Gerd Stamp, himself a decorated bomber pilot. He recalled:

> In April 1943 I was posted to a desk job in Berlin, and it was there that I met "Hajo" Herrmann. Having already flown several hundred sorties I was enjoying a period of rest. I knew that Herrmann had taken to practicing night interceptions. Bomber Command were sending machines over Berlin with increasing frequency and while people said that a Messerschmitt Bf 109 could not be flown at night he

> simply said, "We'll see" When I heard he wanted pilots I asked him if I could join him. I already had the Ritterkreuz so I could fly. However, I had never flown the Bf 109 before. What sort of a man was he? At first, I didn't like him—self-confident, assured, aloof and arrogant. He thought everyone should be able to fly as well as he could.

The first operational intercept flown by Herrmann's pilots took place at around midnight on the night of May 13/14. Fw. Hans Müller got airborne in Fw 190 "CM+CK" and headed out over the northwestern suburbs of Berlin as Mosquito intruders again headed for the capital. Müller returned to Brandenburg-Briest an hour later having failed to spot anything. Two other pilots had made visual contact and opened fire on the elusive Mosquitoes with no result. Fw. Eberhard Brandt filed a claim for an "enemy twin damaged" which was left "pending."

The first relatively successful interception of a British heavy bomber raid employing the *Wilde Sau* tactic did not place until the night of July 3/4 during an attack on Cologne.

It was Müller who "officially" opened the "scoreboard" of the NJVK, Herrmann's men downing 12 bombers from a huge force of 653 bombers. Given the "horse-trading" that went on, six of these were eventually credited to the Flak batteries.

Fw 190 A-2 coded "CM+CK" WNr. 312 flew with the NJVK set up in April 1943 to trial nighttime interceptions of RAF bombers and Mosquitos with single-engined fighters. As soon became very apparent, flying a single-engined fighter at night was a particularly hazardous assignment.

Two views of Uffz. Fritz Rumpelhardt, Schnaufer's radio operator, seen here in the early summer of 1943 in front of and in the rear cockpit of Schnaufer's Bf 110 G-4 in Saint-Trond. Note the augmented armament—in addition to four MG 17s on the nose with two 2-cm guns as standard, it has an additional M1 pod of two MG 151/20s under the belly, which Schnaufer, as Technical Officer of II./NJG 1, may have been testing. The radar array on the nose with vertical dipoles is the FuG 202. After the RAF successfully began jamming the FuG 202 frequency in July 1943, the new FuG 220 radar which was immune to RAF jamming was hastily developed during the summer of 1943.

The Heinkel 219—A Missed Opportunity

The RAF's strategic night bombing of Germany along with the introduction of its four-engined heavy bombers, the Stirling, Halifax, and Lancaster, into Bomber Command, led directly to a 1942 specification issued by Kammhuber for a dedicated night fighter for home-defense duties. Junkers, Messerschmitt, Heinkel, and Tank from Focke Wulf all submitted proposals. The basis for all new designs was the improved Lichtenstein SN-2 search radar, a unit that required an enlarged antenna array, the so-called *Grosse Hirschgeweih*. Messerschmitt opted for a development of the classic Bf 110 with the transition to the Bf 110 G-4/R3, the type with which Schnaufer scored most of his successes. Junkers came up with a new series of the Ju 88, which was more like the Ju 188. This was the Ju 88 G. Kurt Tank submitted a new design in the Ta 154, while Heinkel put forward the He 219. Among other features it had a nose wheel configuration developed at a time when taildraggers were the norm (as did Heinkel's He 280 jet fighter).

With input from some of the leading night fighter aces who spent time at Rostock Mairenehe, the He 219 was, in Kammhuber's view, the most promising design. Powered by two DB 603 A engines developing 1750 hp at takeoff (later the DB 603 G) and various armament configurations featuring at least four MG 151/20 cannon, the He 219 could reach 9,300 meters at 615 kph. But with development and production plagued by infighting and uncertainties, as one German historian put it, "the development of the He 219 was to play out like a tragedy on a par with that of the Me 262."

Following the first flight of the He 219 V1 ("VG+LW") on November 6, 1942, with Heinkel test pilot Gotthold Peter at the controls, no fewer than 38 test and trials (*Versuchs*) machines were constructed. While prototypes featured—or were intended to feature—remote-controlled gun barbettes, ejection seats, and other exotic innovations, most of these developments had been dropped by the time the type entered service. The He 219 was nonetheless fast, heavily armed, had reasonably effective radar and offered outstanding visibility and safety to its crews due to the tricycle undercarriage and ejection seats as detailed in and according to an official 1. Jagddivision report compiled from interviews of I./NJG 1 personnel.

Any new machine entering frontline service experiences teething issues—but in Germany the development and entry into service of new aircraft was always particularly fraught. The RLM did not begin to set up a development planning system until the fall of 1940. Many types had been created after 1936 and then either canceled or mothballed as defects became apparent. Some aircraft types, such as the Junkers Ju 88, only had their defects ironed out years later. So, it was with Heinkel's He 219. The crossfire and sniping soon got underway as the vested interests took positions. As in many other cases, the Secretary of State and the head of the RLM could not bring themselves to make the clear decision that the precarious situation required. Milch always preferred the Ju 188—he regularly flew one as his personal transport. Repeatedly urged by Göring and Hitler to prioritize aircraft production over the development of newer models, a slightly modified version of an aircraft already in series production—the Ju 88 G or the Ju 388—was always likely to boost production figures while in theory performing just as well. Development of a new and "immature" model that had not yet been sufficiently tested was inevitably at the expense of ongoing production—the débâcle of the Me 210 was a good example.

Yet against this background Kammhuber remained a fervent supporter of the He 219, from which he expected more. The RLM demanded a series of comparison flight tests or "flyoffs." The decisive *Vergleichsfliegen* (flyoff) took place over two days at the Rechlin test center on March 25/26, 1943, with Maj. Werner Streib, Kommandeur of I./NJG 1 flying the He 219 V 1 against a Ju 188 E. The He 219 was faster, more maneuverable and could out turn the Ju 188 in a dogfight with its handling described as "*in Ordnung*" (satisfactory). Although this was not perhaps a decisive outcome, it was good enough to order the type to Venlo to be flown under operational conditions. From Rechlin, the Stab I./NJG 1 in Holland received three preproduction A-0s (the V7, the V8, and the V9) for operational testing during May 1943. All three were similarly armed with two MG 151/20s in the wing roots and four 3-cm Mk 108 cannon in the ventral weapons bay. Few if any He 219s ever mounted the Mk 103 cannon. The aircraft were fitted with the FuG 202 Lichtenstein radar.

The destructive start to the He 219's night-fighting career with I./NJG 1 is well known. With his BF Uffz. Helmut Fischer, Streib flew He 219 V9 WNr. 190009 (coded "G9+FB") on its first operational interceptions on the night of June 11/12, 1943, and during a two-hour-long sortie was vectored onto no fewer than five RAF "heavies," resulting in the deaths of over 30 RAF aircrew. Following a malfunction of the landing flaps on approach, the aircraft broke up in the crash that ensued, the crew fortunate to escape unscathed. But the RLM and Dessau (Junkers) soon got wind of the accident and continued to build their case against the He 219 although modest orders for 100, followed by a further 200, machines had already been placed.

A rare view—recently scanned from a long-lost photo negative strip—of a Heinkel He 219 of NJG 1 displaying the Nachtjagd badge under the cockpit and toting a first-generation FuG 220 and centrally mounted short-range FuG 202 antennae.

This 2./NJG 1 aircraft is reported to have crashed in Bergen, Netherlands, shortly after takeoff.

Despite the dangers of flying, there were some moments of relaxation. At Saint-Trond, Hptm. von Bonin (6./NJG 1) plays cards with Ofw. Rudolf Lüdecke, radio operator of his comrade in II./NJG 1, Ofw. Fritz Schellwat.

Lancaster ED781 of 57 Sqn shot down by Oblt. Wilhelm Telge at Lantin, near Liège, on the night of June 24/25, one of 34 losses (out of 630 aircraft involved) in a raid on Wuppertal.

Although, due to bad weather, the first 10 days of June saw no casualties on either side, the fighting remained fierce in June on the Ruhr Front. The Nachtjagd lost 11 aircraft and several crews. In return, 237 victories (including three B-17s) were confirmed to the night fighters.

On the night of June 21/22, 705 bombers attacked Krefeld, 38 of all types (Wellington, Lancaster, Halifax, and Stirling) being shot down. However, the Bf 110 G-4 of Hptm. Manfred Meurer of 3./NJG 1 (who was credited with two victories that night) fell victim to machine-gun fire. The crew was able to bail out over Elsendorp, but the pilot was injured. It was also in the Netherlands that another Ritterkreuzträger, Hptm. Eckart-Wilhelm von

June 20, 1943, at Venlo, Kammhuber's HQ—Herget ("*Der Kleine*") and Frank are awarded the Ritterkreuz.

Bonin of 6./NJG 1 (which had just returned his 16th victory), had to crash-land his damaged "Gustav" at Kloster Achel, with both occupants injured.

Three Ritterkreuze were awarded this month: on June 1 to Hptm. Herbert Lütje (Kommandeur IV./NJG 6); on June 20 to Hptm. Wilhelm Herget (Kommandeur I./NJG 4) and Hans-Dieter Frank (Staka of 2./NJG 1).

A new Gruppe appeared in June: V./NJG 6 commanded by Maj. Paul Semrau and based at Stuttgart-Nellingen. Here too, all the flying personnel were to come from flight schools. The following month, V./NJG 6 was renamed III./NJG 2.

German night-fighting had been unable to develop in the Mediterranean in previous years, due to a lack of resources and, above all, of infrastructure for spotting the enemy and guiding interceptor aircraft. By the end of 1942, the situation had worsened following the British offensive in Egypt (El Alamein) and the American landings in Morocco and Algeria. At the beginning of 1943, the Italo-Germans were fighting vigorously in Tunisia, but this was the last Axis stronghold on African soil.

At the beginning of January 1943, most of the Ju 88 C-6s of I./NJG 2 were equipped with FuG 202 Lichtenstein aircraft and, in February, the Stab NJG 2 along with 2. and 3. Staffeln departed Melsbroek for Castelvetrano in Sicily. There, a 1./NJG 2—the old one had become 10./NJG 3—was reconstituted. II./NJG 2 was still present in Comiso.

Combat in the Mediterranean was very disappointing for NJG 2. As night fighters they were most often used again as *Mädchen für alles* given the Luftwaffe's numerical inferiority in the sector. Moreover, with the Axis having lost control of the air, NJG 2 was regularly bombed on its airfields.

During its five-month presence in the south, NJG 2 scored 19 victories, while Ju 88 losses were in the region of 40 (most often because of bombing). One of the hardest losses was that of Hptm. Dr. Horst Patuschka, Kommandeur of II./NJG 2 and holder of 23 *Nachtabschüsse* (including four in the Mediterranean). His Ju 88 suffered an engine failure

Wreckage of a I./NJG 2 Ju 88 crashed on a beach near Castelvetrano.

Eine größere Liebe hat niemand,
als wer ſein Leben hingibt
für ſeine Freunde.

Zur frommen Erinnerung
im Gebete an
Joſef Mohr
von Ingolſtadt,
Feldw. und Bordmechaniker im Fliegerkorps,
geboren am 4. Januar 1918,
gefallen am 18. April 1943

O liebe Eltern mein
Ich kehre nicht mehr zu Euch Lieben heim,
Der letzte Gedanke, der letzte Blick,
Der eilte noch zu Euch zurück.
Als ich ſtarb im Feindesland,
Reichte niemand mir die Hand;
Doch eh' mein Auge war gebrochen,
Sah ich ſchon den Himmel offen.

DRUCK: L. STADELMEIER, INGOLSTADT

Fw. Mohr was flight engineer/gunner in the crew of Ju 88 C-6 "R4+KL" shot down by a Beaufighter near Cap Bon while escorting aircraft supplying the Tunisian pocket.

and Patuschka was killed with his crew on the night of March 6/7, 1943, near Bizerte. He was posthumously awarded the Ritterkreuz.

Under pressure, I. and II./NJG 2 evacuated Sicily on May 23 to Aquino on the mainland (near Monte Cassino). On July 10, with the Allies having landed in Sicily (Operation *Husky*), NJG 2 returned to Germany (Parchim), where the Ju 88 Cs would be more useful in the defense of the Reich.

July was to prove an important turning point and a major warning for German antiaircraft defenses. From July1 to 24, the Nachtjagd lost nine aircraft, but was only credited with 63 victories, a low figure that was to be explained by the events of the last week of the month.

On July 8, a new IV./NJG 101 was raised at Kitzingen. There must have been a shortage of crews because the new 10. Staffel was formed from 8. Staffel while 11. and 12. Staffeln were made up of neophytes.

On July 24, Bomber Command ended its "battle of the Ruhr." According to J. Alwyn Phillips:

> During the 141 nights and days of the "Battle of the Ruhr" from 5/6 March to 24 July 1943, Bomber Command operated for 61 nights (bombing) and 69 nights (mining) dropping some 45,658 tonnes of bombs in 20,837 night sorties.

July 1943 saw an important change at the head of NJG 1. Obst. Wolfgang Falck, who had led the Geschwader since its formation three years earlier, handed over his post as Kommodore to his great comrade, Ob. Werner Streib. Streib is seen here in Deelen "firing" Falck from the unit.

In July, Hptm. Walter Barte (4./NJG 1), airborne from Saint-Trond, was hit by a bomber's defensive fire and had to crash-land his Bf 110. Both pilot and radio operator were unhurt.

On the night of July 13/14, a Do 217 of 7./NJG 4 from Juvincourt suffered engine trouble while on patrol over southern Belgium. The crew bailed out safely, but the twin-engined aircraft crashed into a house in the hamlet of Chenois (Saint-Léger), killing two civilians.

This Battle of the Ruhr marked the beginning of the RAF's intensive bombing campaign over Germany and, in this relatively short period, the cost was very high. 981 aircraft of all types were lost on bombing missions and 64 on mine-laying missions.

During the last days of July 1943, Allied air activity was much reduced in preparation for Operation *Gomorrah*, a campaign of seven air raids on Hamburg. The aim was the destruction of the city in order both to demoralize the civilian population and to knock out German military-industrial capacity. It was—along with the later bombing of Dresden—the most destructive and deadliest series of air raids in Europe and cost the lives of at least 45,000. According to the plan drawn up on May 27, the RAF and USAAF were to act jointly. The bombardment was carried out over a period of nine days, involving more than 2,593 British bombers who dropped 8,344 tons of bombs at night and around 300 American bombers who led the daytime attacks, dropping 300 tons of bombs.

July 24, 1943, 23:00. The Freya radar beams from the German station in Ostende made contact with the first bombers heading out over the North Sea and communicated this to the bunker HQ of 2. Jagddivision on the airfield at Stade (Lower Saxony). With the Pathfinders out in front and the stream some 200 miles long and 20 miles wide, this huge phalanx droned towards its target—Hamburg, Germany's second largest city located at the mouth of the Elbe and a center of U-boat construction. In the bunker at Stade (Divisional HQ) this huge force was represented as points of light moving slowly across a huge transparent glass wall on which was marked out a map of Germany with the *Himmelbett* grid pattern of night fighter boxes. As the enemy bombers approached, the situation in the air was constantly updated. The deft hands of a dozen or so female Signals auxiliaries, each linked by telephone to a radar station, moved counters representing enemy formations and German night fighter formations. From the other side of the transparent wall, the officers of the fighter command were seated in several rows. Sitting behind them, on raised desks, sat the Divisional Commander, Generalleutnant Walter Schwabedissen, responsible for the air defense for the whole of northwestern Germany. Alongside him were the officers in charge of liaison with fighter unit bases and the Signals Department. NJG 3's Bf 110s and Ju 88s were airborne from Stade, Vechta, Wittmundhafen, Wunstorf, Lüneburg, and Karstrup, and took up position in their respective "boxes" over the German coastline, closely monitored by radar. What would the stream do—turn south for Kiel or Lübeck? Or continue over the Baltic towards a yet unknown goal—Berlin?

Suddenly, Stade HQ was abuzz with activity. The points of light that had been moving on the glass wall a minute earlier suddenly froze. The signals officer telephoned the radar stations. The answer was the same everywhere: equipment not functioning due to some form of jamming … the Freya radars, which operated on a wavelength of 2.40 m, were also "infected," but despite everything, they were still able to distinguish the echo of the bombers from that caused by the jamming. On the other hand, the Würzburgs, operating at 53 cm, recorded on their scopes a mass of returns like a swarm of insects, every "echo" blending. Meanwhile, over the Bay of Germany, 92 million sheets of tinfoil—each strip 27 cm long and 2 cm wide—floated quietly to the ground on the wind. For the Luftwaffe the situation was dramatic—a successful fighter interception depended on the guidance received from the Würzburgs. Fighter controllers were unable to direct anything from the ground. The night fighters continued to orbit aimlessly in the dark, their onboard search radar also unusable. Where was the enemy? Peter Spoden of II./NJG 5—undergoing his *Feuertaufe* (baptism of fire)—knew where they were. Airborne from Parchim, he could see them:

> I was in Raum "Reiher" in the vicinity of Lübeck—one of the last to be sent aloft. I could already see terrible fires raging to the West. *So etwas hatte ich noch nie gesehen*—I'd never seen anything like it. *Mein Gott, sollte das Hamburg sein?* Was that Hamburg burning? Yet I was more than 100 km away. There was interference on the Lichtenstein, no legible returns … Away in the distance I could see four-engined bombers that stood out against the cloud cover glowing brightly from the fires on the ground. *Klein wie Motten*—as small as moths but unmistakable. *Führen Sie mich dahin! Ich kann die Tommies sehen!* I could see them! I instructed the controller to give me a vector towards the bombers. He could not—it was outside of his zone. He ordered me to stay in "Reiher." Enemy aircraft were expected to fly through.

Thanks to Window that night only around 10 bombers were brought down by the night fighters.

On the afternoon of the 25th, a single B-17 (from a force of 122 aircraft) fell to Lt. Gerhard Dittmann of 12./NJG 1 for his first victory. He was to die in combat a month later, on the night of August 17/18. On the night of 25th/26th, the *Wilde Sau* was committed and 18 victories claimed (including three by the single-engined fighters). On the 26th, two B-17s were credited to the Nachtjäger (including Dittmann's second *Abschuss*). On the night of 26th/27th, attacks were more limited, with a single Halifax shot down by a young pilot from 12./NJG 3.

The fourth raid, on July 27/28, 1943, was the most deadly, planned to maximize casualties and material damage. The extreme heat released by the fires created a phenomenon known as the *Feuersturm* (firestorm): a powerful blast mixing air and the flammable gases released by combustion, which spread the fire over 21 km^2 of the city. Tens of thousands of inhabitants were killed, burned or asphyxiated, including in the air-raid shelters. Some 739 bombers were reportedly involved, but only 16 of them were shot down by the Nachtjagd (including four by the JG Herrmann).

In Leeuwarden, three (present and future) Ritterkreuzträger of 11./NJG 1: Oblt. Hermann Greiner (talking with a subordinate), Hptm. Joachim Jabs (note his Crete armband, recalling his time with ZG 76), and the latter's radioman, Erich Weissflog. During Operation *Gomorrah*, Greiner and Jabs were each able to shoot down a Halifax.

On July 29/30, 726 bombers hit the Barmbek district, losing 34 of their number to night fighters who seemed to have recovered somewhat: 16 of these victories were attributed to JG Herrmann.

But Hamburg was not the only German city targeted by Bomber Command at the end of the month. On the night of July 30/31, probably to divide the German forces, 264 bombers were sent to Remscheid; 18 victories were claimed (although only 15 RAF losses were reported). JG Herrmann took the lion's share that night with 14 claims. Between July 25 and 30, the Nachtjagd lost just three aircraft in combat.

Far from these desperate engagements over burning cities, the night of July 28/29 saw the disappearance of the Ju 88 flown by 17-victory ace Oblt. Wolfgang Schneeweiss. A former reconnaissance pilot, he was attached to the Nachtjägdschwarm of Luftflottenkommando 6—one of the first night fighter units attached to local commands on the Eastern Front. Lost in a strafing attack on a group of partisans in the Vitebsk sector, he was posthumously awarded the Ritterkreuz and promoted to Hauptmann. On the same night Hptm. Walter Fenske of 11./NJG 5 downed a DB-3 in the Orel area for his 15th victory, his only Abschuss in the East. IV./NJG 5 had shifted to the Russian Front in early 1943 under Wittgenstein who achieved as many as 20 of his victories flying modified Ju 88 Cs between April and August 1943, before being posted back to the West. By this stage of the war in the East the Soviets were starting to create difficulties for the Germans, specialising in harassment sorties with elderly biplanes. The Polikarpov Po-2, known to the Germans as the "Nähmaschine" (sewing machine) or "UvD" (Unteroffizier von Dienst, or Duty NCO), did little damage in night raids, but was an immense nuisance. During June 1943, Staffeln of IV./NJG 5 were probably based at Briansk and Gomel, being assigned to L.Fl. 4 and 6 for the Kursk offensive "Zitadelle," operating in the Smolensk and Poltava sectors. That summer IV./NJG 5 was renamed I./NJG 100—a new Nachtjagd Geschwader established for night-fighting in the East.

Eastern Front "air fleets" were gradually assigned small detachments of Bf 110/Ju 88s engaged mainly in anti-partisan operations and tasked with hunting down the small aircraft flying nighttime resupply missions for partisan groups. This Bf 110, displaying the code 8V, operated within the Nachtjagdschwarm of Luftflottenkommando 6.

Nachtjagd Units, July 1943

Stab/NJG 1: Deelen

I./NJG 1: Venlo

II./NJG 1: Saint-Trond

III./NJG 1: Twente

IV./NJG 1: Leeuwarden

Stab/NJG 2: Aquino (then Parchim)

I./NJG 2: Aquino (then Parchim)

II./NJG 2: Aquino (then Parchim)

III./NJG 2: Nellingen

Stab/NJG 3: Stade

I./NJG 3: Vechta

II./NJG 3: Schleswig

III./NJG 3: Stade

IV./NJG 3: Grove

Stab/NJG 4: Metz

I./NJG 4: Florennes

II./NJG 4: Saint-Dizier

III./NJG 4: Juvincourt

IV./NJG 4: Mainz-Finthen

Stab/NJG 5: Döberitz

I./NJG 5: Stendal

II./NJG 5: Parchim

III./NJG 5: Neuruppin

IV./NJG 5: Insterburg

IV./NJG 6: Otopeni/Zilistea

Stab/NJG 101: Schleissheim

I./NJG 101: Ingolstadt

II./NJG 101 : Lechfeld

III./NJG 101 : Echterdingen

IV./NJG 101: Kitzingen

Afterword

By mid-1943, Germany was being bombed around the clock. While the effectiveness of this offensive is often called into question, the evidence suggests that in the first six months of 1943 the Wehrmacht devoted 29 percent of its entire weapons and armaments budget to Flak guns (see, for example, Iredale's recent account in *The Pathfinders*). By June 1943, German cities were defended by 1,089 heavy Flak batteries comprising up to 12 guns each, and 738 light Flak batteries with 350 searchlight batteries operated by thousands of German soldiers. An estimated 322 RAF bombers fell to Flak in the three months to July 1943. And while the Nachtjagd had some 400 aircraft available, an inexperienced night fighter pilot needed as many as 50 operational flights to return a "kill." One the most important technical innovations introduced by the Nachtjagd was then undergoing development—*Schräge Musik* or upward-firing cannon. This enabled a night fighter to slowly position itself under a bomber, almost certainly unseen by a tail gunner before delivering the coup de grâce.

Despite this, Bomber Command effectively blinded Kammhuber's defenses over Hamburg—the city was razed and the death toll was horrendous. 23-year-old Bf 110 pilot Wilhelm Johnen was another Nachtjäger airborne in defense of Hamburg on July 27, 1943. Thanks to the deployment of Window, Johnen had—in his rage and frustration—found himself heading towards Amsterdam: "it was obvious no one knew exactly where the enemy was or what his objective would be … how could our defenses have been rendered so impotent." The huge destruction and loss of life, had, as Johnen put it, "the effect of a red light on the German people. Now was the time to capitulate to avoid further damage." The Germans had known about Window since mid-1942 but were horrified by the possibility that the British would discover it and use it to jam their *Himmelbett* system. As Randall Hansen put it, "in one of the war's ironies, British 'angels' were prepared to go where German 'devils' feared to tread." Hamburg was merely the first in a long chain of horrendous attacks that inflicted huge losses on German civilians. The Germans would eventually counter Window—Window of course made no difference to Herrmann and his *Wilde Sau* pilots. Although he maintained his pilots were not ready, his unguided single-seaters downed some 15 RAF bombers over the week of raids that followed July 24. In some ways the Germans benefited from Window—*Zahme Sau* (tame boar) was developed as a counter. In other words, rather than orbiting uselessly around beacons in their rigid boxes, the night fighters would henceforth be introduced into the bomber stream with the Y-Verfahren as early as possible.

References and Further Reading

Becker, Hans-Jürgen. *Schwere Jäger und Zerstörer der Luftwaffe* (Motorbuch, 1999).

Boiten, Theo. *The Nachtjagd War Diaries* (2 vols, Red Kite, 2008), personal accounts translated by Neil Page.

Bundrock, Kurt. *Kampf am nächtlichten Himmel, Einsatzerlebnisse eines Ritterkreuzträgers der Nachtjagd* (Rastatt, 1979). Translated by Neil Page.

Engau, Fritz. *Frontal durch die Bomberpulks* (Grax, Hoppe, 1997).

Falck, Wolfgang. *Falkenjahre—Erinnerungen 1910–2003* (296 Verlag, 2003).

Ferguson, R. *Heinkel He 219: An Illustrated History of the Third Reich's Dedicated Home-Defence Nightfighter* (Red Kite, 2022).

Lorant, Jean-Yves. *Jagdgeschwader 300* (2 vols, Eagle Editions, 2005), translated by Neil Page.

Matthews, J. & Foreman, J. *Luftwaffe Aces* (4 vols, Red Kite 2014).

Mölenbeck, Otto. *Ferne Nachtjagd* (Motorbuch, 1978).

Obermaier, Ernst. *Die Ritterkreuzträger der Luftwaffe 1939–1945* (Dieter Hoffmann, 1966).

Page, Neil. *Luftwaffe Fighters: Combat on All Fronts* (2 vols, Mortons, 2021).

Ries, Karl & Obermaier, Ernst. *Bilanz am Seitenleitwerk* (Dieter Hoffmann, 1970).

Roba, Jean-Louis & Craciunoiu, Cristian. *La Chasse de Nuit allemande en Roumanie* (Bucharest, 1994).

Roba, Jean-Louis. *The Luftwaffe in Africa* (Casemate, 2019).

Roba, Jean-Louis & Taghon, Peter. *La Luftwaffe en Belgique* (2 vols, Lela Presse, 2021).

Roba, Jean-Louis. *La Luftwaffe en France 1939–45* (2 vols, Éditions Arès, 2022).

Saintes, Philippe. *Luftwaffe Victory Markings 1939–45* (Casemate, 2022).

Spoden, Peter. *Ich war Nachtjäger in Göring's Luftwaffe* (self-published, 2007).

Stipdonk, P. & Meyer, M. *Die Deutsche Luftwaffe—Zerstörer- und Nachtjägerverbände* (4 vols, VDM Heinz Nickel).

Zorner, Paul. *Nächte im Bomberstrom: Erinnerungen 1920–1950* (NeunundzwanzigSechs-Verlag, 2007).

Various issues of *Jägerblatt* (journal of the German fighter pilots association), including the "Fernnachtjäger" series by Mölenbeck and the II./NJG 1 war diary by Diener.

Various Bundesarchiv RL/10 files.

Index

Aalborg, 8, 11, 13–14, 103
Altendorf, Rudolf, 107
Alten-Rheine, 68
Amsterdam-Schiphol, 14
Athens, 73
Athies, 62, 76, 79–80, 87, 96
Autenrieth, Hans, 61, 77–79

Bardia, 74
Barmbek, 122
Barmen-Wuppertal, 106
Barte, Walter, 118
Becker, Ludwig, 34, 41, 57, 76, 90, 92
Becker, Martin, 99
Beier, Wilhelm, 42, 46, 100
Benghazi, 36, 73
Bennett's Pathfinders, 89
Berlin, 6, 10, 24, 53, 58, 77, 90, 108–110, 120
Bismarck, 30–31
Böhme, Gerhard, 31, 47
Bohn, Paul, 18, 30, 32
Bonin, Eckart-Wilhelm von, 30, 61, 114, 116
Bonn-Hangelar, 10, 109
Bönsch, Herbert, 18, 62, 76
Borchers, Walter, 51, 102
Born, Ludwig, 33
Bothmer, Conrad von, 14, 20
Brandenburg-Briest, 10, 110
Brandt, Eberhard, 110
Bremen, 40, 73, 102
Brest, 31, 59
Bruneval, capture of Würzburg radar system at, 7, 57, 104
Brussels, 73, 75
Bucharest-Otopeni, 105, 106, 123
Bundrock, Kurt, 27, 41–42, 54, 75–76, 100

Cap Bon, 117
Casablanca Conference, 89
Castelvetrano, 116
Catania, 36, 50
"Channel Dash" *see* Operation *Donnerkeil*
Churchill, Winston, 89
Cologne, attack on, 7, 52, 66, 110
Comiso, 87, 116
Condor Legion, 10, 15, 56, 71, 103
Coulommiers, 78
Cunningham, John, 44

D-Day, 78
Deelen, 15, 19, 24, 50, 55, 72, 87, 118, 123
Defection from NJG 3, 103
Derna, 36, 73
Deutsche Afrika Korps, 24, 36
Dietrich, Otto, 12
Dittmann, Gerhard, 121
Döberitz, 10, 79, 87, 123
Dortmund, 106
Douhet, Guilio, 10
Dresden, bombing of, 119
Drewes, Martin, 48
Dunkelnachtjagd sorties, 25, 27, 41, 48, 66
Düsseldorf, 15–16

Eckardt, Reinhold, 31, 43, 59, 62, 75–76
Ehle, Walter, 14, 17, 19–20, 25, 56, 71, 101
El Alamein, 7, 73, 89, 116
Engels, Johannes, 98–99
Essen, raid on, 59–60, 69, 93

Falck, Wolfgang, 6, 11–12, 14, 16–17, 19–22, 33, 46, 54, 118
Fall Gelb, 56
Fenske, Walter, 27, 31, 122
Fernnachtjagd sorties, 18, 22, 29, 33, 39, 47–48, 86, 100
Feuersturm (firestorm) raids, 7, 121
Fick, Werner, 35
Fischer, Helmut, 113
Florennes, 61, 79–81, 87, 96, 101, 123
Focke Wulf, 112
Förster, Hermann, 11, 17, 52
Frank, Heinz-Dieter,
Freya radar system, 6, 11–12, 24, 48, 52–53, 73, 120
FuG 202 radar *see* Lichenstein radar system
FuG 220 radar, 111, 113
Funkfeuer radio beacon, 52

Gibson, Guy, 30
Giessübel, Vincenz, 34
Gildner, Paul, 27–28, 35, 40, 48, 50, 92
Gilze-Rijen, 18–19, 21, 27, 30–31, 34, 39, 46–47, 50, 62, 83, 86, 92, 103, 108
Göring, Hermann, 14, 40, 112
Greiner, Hermann, 121
Griese, Heinrich, 43
Grove, 83–84, 87, 123
Gütersloh, 15
Gutezeit, Fritz, 65–66

Hahn, Hans, 30, 37, 39–40, 47

Hamburg, 7, 9, 24, 27, 41, 92, 119–120, 122, 124
Harris, Arthur "Bomber," 52, 57–58, 65–66, 69, 75, 87, 89
Heinkel, 112
Helbig, Georg, 77–78
Helle Nachtjagd, 17, 21, 48, 53, 55, 73, 109
Helle Riegel, 52
Helmer, Karl, 76
Herget, Wilhelm, 38, 48, 51, 59, 61, 65, 76, 79–80, 101, 115–116
Hermann, Hans, 43, 72
Herrick, Michael, 32
Herrmann, Hans-Joachim "Hajo," 108–110, 124
Herrmann, Kurt, 19, 27
Heyse, Karl-Heinrich, 14–15, 18, 21
Hiltrop, August, 31–32, 47
Himmelbett system, 9, 40, 96, 98, 120, 124
Hitler, Adolf, 6, 10, 47, 73, 112
Holler, Kurt, 65, 76
Huhn, Hans, 92
Hülshoff, Karl-Theodor "Kurt," 18, 21

Insterburg, 90, 123

Jabs, Hans-Joachim, 51, 121
Jafü Süddeutschland, 90
Jever, 10
Johanssen, Karl, 98–99
Jung, Erich, 73
Jung, Rudolf "Rolf," 18, 25
Junkers, 33, 103, 112–113
Juvincourt, 76, 80, 87, 119, 123

Kammhuber Line, 6, 8, 23–24, 48, 62, 73, 124
Kammhuber, Josef, 6, 8–9, 18, 23–24, 33, 40, 46, 48, 63, 86, 112–113, 115
Kanal Durchbruch see Operation *Donnerkeil*
Karstrup, 120
Kastelli airfield, Crete, 73–74
Kennel, Karl, 49
Kesselring, Albert, 21
Kiel, 35, 41, 120
Kitzingen, 49–50, 117, 123
Knacke, Reinhold, 22, 27–28, 41–42, 50, 52–54, 59, 75–76, 90, 92–93
Knickmeier, Walter, 52
Knoetzsch, Hans-Dietrich, 93
Kollak, Reinhard, 43, 72
Költringer, Christian, 98
König, Hans-Heinrich, 51
Köster, Alfons, 82–83, 86
Krefeld, 115
Kuthe, Wolfgang, 89–90

Launer, Richard, 59
Laupheim, 65
Lechfeld, 83, 90, 123
Leeuwarden, 48, 50, 83, 87, 96, 108, 121, 123
Lent, Helmut, 19, 31, 38, 43, 58–59, 73, 83, 96, 106
Lettenmeier, Wilhelm, 30
Lichtenstein radar system (FuG 202), 6, 33–34, 38, 48, 53–55, 57, 60, 64, 72–73, 88, 92, 98–99, 103–104, 111–113, 116, 120
Li-Gerät *see* Lichtenstein radar system
Lippe-Weissenfeld, Egmont Prinz zur, 21, 27, 48, 50, 59, 65, 85, 93
Loos, Kurt, 22
Lübeck, 120
Lüneburg, 120
Lütje, Herbert, 59, 105–106, 116

Mainz-Finthen, 65, 90, 98, 123
Malta, 36, 73–74
Mau, Paul, 31–32
Meijel, 52
Meister, Ludwig, 80, 96
Messerschmitt, 112
Metz, 87, 123
Meurer, Manfred, 53, 102, 115
Milch, Erhard, 29, 112
Möhlenbeck, Otto, 30, 37
Mölders, Viktor, 16–17
Monica tail-warning radar, 9
Müller, Hans, 10, 110
Münchengladbach, 14, 56
Munich-Riem, 36, 93

Nachtjagdversuchskommando Herrmann (NJVK), 109–110
Nacke, Heinz, 48, 51
Neuruppin, 102, 123
Ney, Siegfried, 48
Night Fighter Test Detachment Herrmann *see* Nachtjagdversuchskommando Herrmann (NJVK)
Niklas, Helmut, 66–68
Nugent, Carlos, 74

Oboe bomb aiming and navigation system, 9, 89
Operation *Barbarossa*, 7, 32
Operation *Donnerkeil*, 59, 77
Operation *Gomorrah*, 119, 121
Operation *Husky*, 117
Operation *Merkur*, 36
Operation *Nickel*, 62
Operation *Weserübung*, 6, 11
Oshima, Hiroshi, 51

Ostende, 120
Ostpreussen, 90

Palm, Gerhard, 33
Parchim, 83, 87, 117, 120, 123
Patuschka, Horst, 86, 116–117
Peters, Helmut, 93
Ploiesti oilfields, 105
Pointner, Anton, 12
Prinz Eugen, 59

Radusch, Walter, 12–14, 19
RAF 1,000 bomber raids, 7, 66–67, 69, 73
RAF Bassingbourn, 39
RAF Bomber Command, 6–7, 11, 14, 17, 23, 31, 40–41, 47, 57, 73, 75, 79–80, 89, 93, 106, 109, 112, 117, 122, 124
RAF Dyce, 7, 103–104
RAF Waddington, 19, 26, 34, 52
Rauh, Hubert, 62–63
Rechlin test center, 113
Reese, Hermann, 22
Remscheid, 122
Rheine, 65
Rökker, Heinz, 74
Rommel, Erwin, 24, 36
Roosevelt, F. D., 89
Rossiwall, Theodor, 93
Rostock Mairenehe, 112
Royal Navy (British), 30
Ruhr, battle of the, 7, 89–104, 117
Rumpelhardt, Fritz, 69–70, 111

Saarbrücken, 75
Saint-Dizier, 87, 123
Saint-Trond (Sint-Truiden), 43, 50, 55–56, 60–62, 67–68, 71, 76–77, 79–80, 87, 108, 111, 114, 118, 123
Sayn-Wittgenstein, Heinrich zu, 75, 83
Schäfer, Fritz, 79
Schalk, Johann, 44, 46
Scharnhorst, 59, 77
Schleissheim, 93, 123
Schleswig, 44, 50, 87, 123
Schnaufer, Heinz, 7, 69–70, 73, 111–112
Schneeweiss, Wolfgang, 122
Schoenert, Rudolf, 75–76, 83
Schräge Musik cannon, 6, 9, 96–97, 124
Schumacher, Carl, 12
Schwabedissen, Helmut, 14
Schwabedissen, Walter, 120
Schwarz, Hugo, 33
Semrau, Paul, 26, 32, 82–83, 85–86, 116
Sicily, 24, 36, 47, 73–74, 116–117
Siegmund, Rudolf, 64, 94–95
Simon, Erich, 83–85
Sommer, Hermann, 19, 31, 34
Spies, Walter, 49
Spoden, Peter, 120
Stade, 10, 44, 48, 50, 87, 120, 123
Stamp, Gerd, 109
Steinhoff, Johannes, 10, 12
Stellungen radar positions, 52
Stendal, 79, 87, 123
Stoltenhoff, Rudolf, 93, 95
Streib, Werner, 8, 12–14, 16–17, 19–20, 31, 50, 52–53, 55, 75, 92, 113, 118
Strüning, Heinz, 31, 47, 83, 86
Stuttgart-Echterdingen, 96

Tank, Kurt, 112
Tavaux, 77–78
Telefunken, 53
Telge, Wilhelm, 115
Thimmig, Wolfgang "Ameise," 22
Thomas, Herbert, 103
Training Command East, 100
Trenchard, Hugh, 10
Twente, 50, 87, 123

U-boat construction, 120
Uellenbeck, Gustav, 72
USAAF, 47, 92–93, 119
  Eighth Air Force, 91

Vegesack U-boat yards, 91
Veuklen Nachtjagdgefechtsstand, 8
Vlissingen (Flushing), 19

Wandam, Siegfried, 17, 59, 79
Weissflog, Erich, 121
Wenning, Heinrich(?), 67–68
Westfeldzug Campaign in the West, 35
Wilde Sau, 6–7, 9, 105–124
Wilhelmshaven, 53–94
"Window" (chaff), 6, 104, 121, 124
Wittmundhafen, 83, 120
Wohlers, Heinrich, 90
Würzburg radar system, 6–7, 25, 41, 48, 52–54, 57, 73, 99, 101, 104, 120

Y-Verfahren range-finding system, 55, 124

Zeist, 52
Zeppelin, 10–11
Zilistea, 105, 123
Zipperlein, Kurt, 57
Zone Libre (France), 86
Zorner, Paul, 53, 83, 85, 90–93, 96, 102, 106